THE TAMING OF
THE SHREW

William Shakespeare

Edited by
CEDRIC WATTS

WORDSWORTH CLASSICS

In loving memory of
MICHAEL TRAYLER
the founder of Wordsworth Editions

4

Readers who are interested in other titles from
Wordsworth Editions are invited to visit our website at
www.wordsworth-editions.com

For our latest list and a full mail-order service contact
Bibliophile Books, 5 Thomas Road, London E14 7BN
TEL: +44 (0)20 7515 9222 FAX: +44 (0)20 7538 4115
E-MAIL: orders@bibliophilebooks.com

First published in 1993 by Wordsworth Editions Limited
8B East Street, Ware, Hertfordshire SG12 9HJ

ISBN 978-1-85326-079-7

Text © Wordsworth Editions Limited 2004
Introduction, notes and all other editorial matter
© Cedric Watts, 2004

Wordsworth® is a registered trademark of
Wordsworth Editions Limited

Typeset by Antony Gray
Printed in Great Britain by
Clays Ltd, St Ives plc

CONTENTS

General Introduction	6
Introduction	7
Further Reading	16
Note on Shakespeare	18
Acknowledgements and Textual Matters	19
THE TAMING OF THE SHREW	23
Appendix: The 'Christopher Slie' Material	103
Notes on The Taming of the Shrew	111
Glossary	131

GENERAL INTRODUCTION

In the Wordsworth Classics' Shakespeare Series, the inaugural volumes, *Romeo and Juliet*, *The Merchant of Venice* and *Henry V*, have been followed by *The Taming of the Shrew*, *A Midsummer Night's Dream*, *Much Ado about Nothing*, *Hamlet*, *Twelfth Night*, *Othello* and *King Lear*, and further editions will ensue. Each play in this Shakespeare Series is accompanied by a standard apparatus, including an introduction, explanatory notes and a glossary. The textual editing takes account of recent scholarship while giving the material a careful reappraisal. The apparatus is, however, concise rather than elaborate. We hope that the resultant volumes prove to be handy, reliable and helpful. Above all, we hope that, from Shakespeare's works, readers will derive pleasure, wisdom, provocation, challenges, and insights: insights into his culture and ours, and into the era of civilisation to which his writings have made – and continue to make – such potently influential contributions. Shakespeare's eloquence will, undoubtedly, re-echo 'in states unborn and accents yet unknown'.

CEDRIC WATTS
Series Editor

INTRODUCTION

'*The Shrew* . . . is a macho fantasy for an alcoholic yob.'
'Shakespeare's sympathy with and almost uncanny
understanding of women characters is one of the
distinguishing features of his comedy . . . ' [1]

I

Shakespeare's *The Taming of the Shrew* [2] is a lively, vigorous and
much-adapted play. There have been numerous modern versions
for radio, the cinema and television; it has prompted operas, a
ballet by John Cranko, the musical comedy *You Made Me Love
You* and, of course, *Kiss Me, Kate*, the famous Cole Porter
musical for stage and screen; and it has influenced such diverse
films as John Ford's *The Quiet Man* and Gil Junger's *10 Things I
Hate about You*. It is also a surprisingly ambiguous and highly
controversial work. Accordingly, Part 2 of this introduction, after
discussing source-materials, summarises a case that could be made
against the play; Part 3 offers a defence; and Part 4 provides a
conclusion.

2

The Taming of the Shrew is certainly one of Shakespeare's early
comedies; possibly, according to some scholars, his earliest.[3] It
may have been written between 1590 and 1592. Shakespeare used
a variety of source-materials for the play. The deception of Sly
has numerous precedents and analogues: for instance, the Arabian
anthology, *The Thousand and One Nights*, contains the story of a
drunken man who is drugged, taken to a palace, and convinced
for a while that he is the ruler.[4] (In Shakespeare's version, when

we first meet Sly, he has been vigorously ejected from a tavern by its hostess, which sheds an ironic light on the display of masculinity in the drama that follows.) The shrew-taming plot derives from a folk-tale tradition. Traditional elements included: a prosperous father with good and bad daughters; warnings to the suitor about the shrew; bizarrely unconventional behaviour at the wedding; the process of taming; a journey to the home of the shrew's father; and the laying of a wager on the bride's conduct.[5] All these elements re-emerge in the play. The plot-material concerning the rival suitors of Bianca derives partly from the Roman comedies of Plautus and Terence, transmitted via Ariosto's *I Suppositi* (1509) and George Gascoigne's *Supposes* (1566). The names 'Grumio' and 'Tranio' can be found in Plautus's *Mostellaria*, while *Supposes* provided the names of Petruchio and Licio. In Act 5, scene 1, of *The Taming of the Shrew*, Vincentio is denied access to his son by an impostor, a pedant posing as Vincentio and abetted by a servant. Precedent for this is found in *Supposes*, Act 4, scenes 4 and 5; and an ancient analogue is provided by Plautus's *Amphitryo*, when the eponymous Amphitryo knocks at the door of his own house and is not allowed to enter: a situation also exploited in Shakespeare's *The Comedy of Errors*. Predictably, *The Taming of the Shrew* employs some perennial 'stock characters': for instance, the clever servant (Tranio), the cheeky page (Biondello), and the elderly suitor or 'pantaloon' in the tradition of the Italian *commedia dell'arte* (Gremio).

In *The Taming of the Shrew*, Shakespeare was ambitious in combining such diverse materials, but the process of transmission has not served his endeavours kindly. This comedy has survived in only incomplete form: we lack, for example, the conclusion of the Christopher Sly material. A different work, *The Taming of a Shrew* (note the '*a*'), does complete the Sly sequence: see the Appendix in this volume. (*The Taming of a Shrew* seems to be a garbled version of Shakespeare's play, a product of recollection and rewriting by others.) Furthermore, a person or persons involved in the copying and/or printing of *The Taming of the Shrew* apparently suffered from deafness to rhythm, and consequently marred the metre of numerous lines. They limp and stumble, when it would have been so easy to keep them steady or put them right. By the way, when confronted by the diversity of suitors, disguises and deceptions in the Bianca plot, you may occasionally become bewildered. If that happens, don't worry: you are not alone. There are signs that Shakespeare himself occasionally got into a muddle, as the notes to this edition demonstrate.[6]

The most controversial part of the work is undoubtedly the 'taming' plot. On the basis of the divisions among its critics, *The Taming of the Shrew* probably deserves to be classed as one of the 'problem plays' of Shakespeare. In 1978, when reviewing a new production, Michael Billington in *The Guardian* referred to the play's 'moral and physical ugliness' and asked 'whether there is any reason to revive a play that seems totally offensive to our age and our society'.[7] Even in Shakespeare's lifetime, this work was evidently disturbing, for it provoked a counterblast from John Fletcher, whose play *The Woman's Prize, or The Tamer Tamed* (*c.* 1611) shows the taming of Petruchio by his second wife. The moral, says its epilogue, is that the two sexes should learn 'to love mutually'.[8] Down the centuries, *The Taming of the Shrew* – particularly Katherina's speech advocating submission to the husband – has offered challenges to directors and critics. In the 18th century, David Garrick influentially adapted the play so that Petruchio renounces 'all Rudeness, Wilfulness, and Noise' and commends 'one gentle Stream / Of mutual Love, Compliance, and Regard'.[9] (Garrick's adaptation, *Catharine and Petruchio*, 1754, appears to have prevailed in England for ninety years.) In 1897, the astute left-wing dramatist, George Bernard Shaw, said of *The Taming of the Shrew*'s last scene:

> No man with any decency of feeling can sit it out in the company of a woman without being extremely ashamed of the lord-of-creation moral implied in the wager and the speech put into the woman's own mouth.[10]

You can easily see that numerous features of the play could give offence. Petruchio arrives 'to wive it wealthily in Padua': he plans to marry for money ('As wealth is burden of my wooing dance'), even if his bride be ugly or old. On hearing that Katherina will bring a rich dowry, he is set on marrying her, although he has not yet seen her. She is termed a 'devil', a 'fiend of hell' and 'the devil's dam'. His wooing, like the wedding, veers between the farcical and the brutal. Since she freely accepts him at the ceremony, the subsequent 'taming' seems gratuitous. Petruchio proceeds to bully and starve his wife, repeatedly contradicting her wishes. If he does not actually hit her, he hits others and frighteningly displays his readiness to be physically violent; and, sickeningly, his wealth and social status enable him to be aggressive with impunity. Katherina is rendered submissive by various forms of intimidation, torture and humiliation. She is deprived of food, of sleep, and of independent thought. If Petruchio says the sun is the moon, she must agree. Eventually, he publicly displays her as a bride who will obey his every whim − so that, after trampling her hat at his command, she makes the long speech which urges all wives to revere their lords and masters. It may bring to mind the Elizabethan 'Homily on Marriage' which Anglican priests read to their congregations and which asserts: '[Y]e women, submit your selues unto your owne husbandes, as unto the Lord. For the husband is the wiues head, euen as Christ is the head of the Church . . . '.[11] Katherina says:

> Thy husband is thy lord, thy life, thy keeper,
> Thy head, thy sovereign; one that cares for thee
> And for thy maintenance . . .
> Such duty as the subject owes the prince,
> Even such a woman oweth to her husband; . . .
> I am ashamed that women are so simple,
> To offer war where they should kneel for peace,
> Or seek for rule, supremacy and sway,
> Where they are bound to serve, love and obey.

We see that she, once a spirited, independent and defiant woman, is not only thoroughly tamed but also manipulated as a means to rebuke other females. She talks of the husband as the diligent and suffering breadwinner, even though, in her case, the husband (who so recently denied her a decent meal) is a rich man made much richer by her dowry. In short, feminists may well recoil from a play which seems aggressively prejudiced against women.

3

A Shakespeare play is not fixed and static; it moves through time, changing in response to changing circumstances, being revised, adapted, and sometimes transformed, by copyists, printers, editors, directors and actors. Some productions of *The Taming of the Shrew* have evoked hostility to Petruchio by emphasising or increasing his harshness. In Charles Marowitz's free adaptation (1973–4), Katherina was driven mad and was brutally raped. Alternatively, productions have emphasised her resilience. Mary Pickford, in a 1929 film version, gave an ironic wink when delivering Katherina's speech on submission, and Vanessa Redgrave in 1961 seemed to add 'a delicious touch of irony' to it. Coppélia Kahn has argued not only that this speech is ironic but also that the play as a whole 'satirizes . . . the male urge to control woman'.[12]

One tricky pair of questions is this: does Katherina actually fall in love with Petruchio, and, if so, when? Some productions suggest that she falls in love with him virtually on sight, so that her apparent resistance can be seen in part as a delaying game entailing degrees of complicity with her wooer. Arguably, his bullying modulates into protracted teasing, as when, on their first night together in a bedchamber, he is heard '[m]aking a sermon of continency to her'. By 4.5.36–40 (when she assures old Vincentio that he will make a 'lovely bedfellow' for some lucky man), she is clearly willing to collaborate resourcefully in Petruchio's schemes of mockery. A serious undercurrent is evident there, in the readiness of both partners to mimic derisively the clichés of the flattering amatory address, as if to suggest that their own stormy progress towards mutuality may be a sounder testing-course for a relationship than is the customary idealising ritual of romantic courtship. Katherina's love for Petruchio is fully confirmed by the end of Act 5, scene 1. Here she addresses him as 'Husband' and 'love'; indeed, kissing him in the street, she says 'Now pray thee, love, stay' – thus, in symbolic harmony, completing a rhyming couplet by echoing Petruchio's 'let's away'. Germaine Greer, an eminent feminist, has commented: 'Kate...has the uncommon good fortune to find Petruchio[,] who is man enough to know what he wants and how to get it'. She adds that 'only Kates make good wives, and then only to Petruchios; for the rest, their cake is dough'. As for the controversial speech on submission, to Greer this is 'the greatest defence of Christian monogamy ever written', as it specifies the husband's rôle as protector and friend.[13] To Marilyn Cooper and Lisa Jardine, however, the speech is extremely ambiguous, and Jardine aptly says:

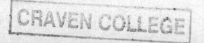

Depending on how we take her tone, Kate is seriously tamed, is ironic at Petruchio's expense, has learned comradeship and harmonious coexistence, or will remain a shrew till her death.[14]

In Shakespeare's theatre, female parts were played by boys. If the apparently submissive Katherina is acted by a boy, does this accentuate the sense of male control (since females are not really present on the stage) or weaken it (since the voice of submission is not really that of a woman)? In 2003 a provocative cultural reversal took place: there was an all-female production at the Globe Theatre in London. Janet McTeer played Petruchio to Kathryn Hunter's Katherina. As McTeer's Petruchio swaggered, blustered and bullied, the effect was to make the play, to a large extent, a satire on aggressive *machismo*. In this case, the controversial speech provoked dawning dismay from the 'male' listeners, while Katherina became increasingly delighted by the power of her own eloquence: their approving nods and sentimental tears gave way to apprehension and alarm. (Of course, different members of an audience may respond diversely to a particular speech, and an actor's or a director's interpretation of a rôle or play may vary during the theatrical run. Nevertheless, when I saw that production, the good-humoured interaction between actors and audience notably mitigated the harsher features of the play.)[15]

That 2003 version eliminated the Christopher Sly material. Productions which include it add another layer of irony, since the main action is then seen as 'a play within a play', an entertainment staged by men as part of the fooling of a man, Christopher himself, who initially was humiliated by a woman, the hostess who ejected him from the tavern. For feminist observers, other complications in *The Taming of the Shrew* include Katherina's bullying of Bianca: there is little evidence of sisterly solidarity. Psychologically and physically, she belabours Bianca, evidently because of her jealous fear that her sister will soon gain a husband while Katherina 'must dance bare-foot on her wedding day' and eventually, like the proverbial spinster, 'lead apes in hell'. On the other hand, much of Petruchio's aggressive blustering is directed against men: he knocks down a priest, strikes servants, abuses the tailor and haberdasher, and generally plays the part of swaggering bully to all and sundry.[16] In a morally balanced comedy, he would eventually be humbled;

in this one, he probably gets away with too much. But people who seek 'morally balanced' comedy will seldom be gratified in the theatre, whether it's the theatre of Aristophanes, of Shakespeare, or of Alan Ayckbourn. The critic Benedict Nightingale has remarked that audiences for *The Taming of the Shrew* may find 'a funny, touching, coarse, romantic, morally confusing mix of sexism and sophistication'; and he adds: 'well, isn't that better than a politically correct nothing-very-much?'.[17]

4

Shakespeare knew Chaucer's *The Canterbury Tales*, that huge sequence in which the related topics of love and marriage are subject to an immensely complex discussion, ranging from the Wife of Bath's defence of her egoistic outlook to the Franklin's emphasis on the value of mutual harmony. Shakespeare, in turn, offers in his plays a wide range of attitudes. Within a few years of *The Taming of the Shrew*, he wrote *Love's Labour's Lost*, a remarkably unconventional comedy in which the lords who woo the ladies are repeatedly humiliated; a comedy which finally does not end with wedding bells at all, but sees the men departing as probationers: here, 'Jack hath not Jill'.[18] Shakespeare could make men seem moon-governed and changeable in their desires, in need of education by women. In *Romeo and Juliet*, Romeo's love for Juliet rapidly supersedes his love for Rosaline, and in Act 2, scene 2, when he seeks to adopt a romantically rhetorical style, he is rebuked by Juliet who, though only thirteen years old, is there more intelligent and practical than he. Whether in a tragedy (*Othello*) or a late romance (*Cymbeline* or *The Winter's Tale*), Shakespeare could show men whose love can easily be poisoned by jealousy and transmuted to murderous hatred. Sometimes a play may seem emphatic about the importance of confining sexual fulfilment to the bounds of holy wedlock: Hermia in *A Midsummer Night's Dream* and, strikingly, Prospero in *The Tempest* are explicit on this matter. Sometimes, however, a play may seem to celebrate the intensity of adulterous sexuality: in *A Midsummer Night's Dream* again, Titania enjoys ineffable bliss with Bottom,[19] while, in *Antony and Cleopatra*, the energetic power of the relationship between the two experienced lovers transcends the cool marital relationship between Antony and his wife Octavia. Shakespeare's sonnets convey the joy and the bitterness not only of love for a man but also of adulterous love for a woman; and one poem in the sequence (number 145, which puns on the name Hathaway) is a reminder of his love for his wife. Germaine Greer has said of Shakespeare:

> He projected the ideal of the monogamous sexual couple so luminously [in his writings] that they irradiate our notions of compatibility and co-operation between spouses to this day.[20]

Nevertheless, though this may be true, other ideals and other possibilities are also irradiated by those writings. *The Taming of the Shrew* is just one part, though a vivid and important part, of Shakespeare's vast exposition of the tensions and complexities of human sexual, amatory and marital relationships.

NOTES TO THE INTRODUCTION

1 Benedict Nightingale: 'The Old Trouble and Strife' in *The Times*, 18 August 2003, Section 2, pp. 8–9; quotation, p. 9. Anne Barton on *The Taming of the Shrew* in *The Riverside Shakespeare*, ed. G. Blakemore Evans *et al.* (Boston: Houghton Mifflin, 1974), pp. 106–9; quotation, p. 107.

2 As the play reminds us at 4.1.195–6 and 5.2.28–9, Shakespeare pronounced 'shrew' to rhyme with 'show' and 'woe'. At 5.2.188 in this edition, it is spelt 'shrow', to match the spelling used there in the earliest text, and rhymes with 'so'. (The pronunciation of 'Kate' varies between 'Kate' and 'Kat'.)

3 See Marcus Mincoff: 'The Dating of *The Taming of the Shrew*' in *English Studies* 54 (1973), pp. 554–65; Brian Morris: 'Introduction' to *The Taming of the Shrew* (London: Methuen, 1981), pp. 50–65.

4 See 'The Tale of the Sleeper Wakened' in *The Book of the Thousand Nights and One Night*, tr. Powys Mathers, Vol. 3 (London: Routledge, n.d., rpt. 1947), pp. 323–74. Robert Burton's *The Anatomy of Melancholy* (Pt 2, section 2) reports the legend that Philippus Bonus, Duke of Burgundy, arranged for a drunken country-fellow to be conveyed to a palace and treated for a day as if he were a duke.

5 J. H. Brunwand: 'The Folktale Origin of *The Taming of the Shrew*' in *Shakespeare Quarterly* 17 (1966), pp. 345–59, notably p. 347. See also: Antti Aarne and Stith Thompson: *The Types of the Folktale* (Helsinki: Suomalainen Tiedeakatemia, 1964), pp. 311–12.

6 See, for example, the notes to 3.2.122, 4.5.61–2, and 5.2.S.D.

7 Michael Billington: 'A Spluttering Firework' in *The Guardian*, 5 May 1978, p. 10.

8 John Fletcher: *The Woman's Prize, or The Tamer Tamed*, ed. G. B. Ferguson (The Hague: Mouton, 1966), p. 148. In 2004, the Royal Shakespeare Company varied its run of *The Taming of the Shrew* by including some performances of *The Tamer Tamed*.

9 David Garrick: *Catharine and Petruchio. A Comedy*: in *The Dramatic Works of David Garrick Esq.*, Vol. 2 (no place or publisher named, 1768), p. 202.

10 George Bernard Shaw: *Shaw on Shakespeare*, ed. Edwin Wilson (London: Cassell, 1962), p. 180.

11 The homily, as quoted here, is part of the 'Fourme of Solemnization of Matrimonie' in the *Booke of Common Prayer* (London, 1584). Though Katherina emphasises submission to the male, she does not go quite as far as to liken the husband to Christ.

12 Charles Marowitz: *The Shrew* in *The Marowitz Shakespeare* (London: Marion Boyars, 1978). On Pickford: E. A. Baughan: 'Doug and Mary in Shakespearean Farce': *Daily News and Westminster Gazette*, 15 November 1929, p. 7. On Redgrave: Tom Milne: 'The Taming of the Director': *Time and Tide*, 21 September 1961, p. 1,564. Coppélia Kahn: *Man's Estate: Masculine Identity in Shakespeare* (Berkeley: University of California Press, 1981), pp. 104–18; quotation, p. 104.

13 Germaine Greer: *The Female Eunuch* (London: McGibbon and Kee, 1970), pp. 209. Her 'cake is dough' phrase wittily echoes an idiom used twice in the play.

14 Lisa Jardine: *Still Harping on Daughters: Women and Drama in the Age of Shakespeare* (Brighton: Harvester, 1983), p. 59.

15 I attended the *matinée* performance on 29 August 2003. The play was directed by Phyllida Lloyd. In the same year, a production at Brighton by Mark Rosenblatt allowed Katherina (played by Nichola McAuliffe) to deliver the controversial speech with evident sincerity.

16 To be fair to Petruchio, it should be noted that he privately tells Hortensio to pay the much-maligned tailor, which suggests that he may covertly compensate some (if not all) of his other male victims.

17 Nightingale: 'The Old Trouble and Strife', p. 9.

18 The long-lost *Love's Labour's Won* probably concluded the story of the courtships. See 'Shakespeare's Feminist Play?' in John Sutherland and Cedric Watts: *Henry V, War Criminal? and Other Shakespeare Puzzles* (Oxford: Oxford University Press, 2000), pp. 174–83.

19 See 'Does Bottom Cuckold Oberon?' in *Henry V, War Criminal? and Other Shakespeare Puzzles*.

20 Germaine Greer: *Shakespeare* (Oxford: Oxford University Press, 1986), p. 124.

FURTHER READING
(in chronological order)

Narrative and Dramatic Sources of Shakespeare, Vol. I, ed. Geoffrey Bullough. London: Routledge and Kegan Paul; New York: Columbia University Press, 1957.

E. M. W. Tillyard: *Shakespeare's Early Comedies*. London: Chatto and Windus, 1965.

Germaine Greer: *The Female Eunuch*. London: McGibbon and Kee, 1970.

Ralph Berry: *Shakespeare's Comedies: Explorations in Form*. Princeton, N.J.: Princeton University Press, 1972.

Leo Salingar: *Shakespeare and the Traditions of Comedy*. London: Cambridge University Press, 1974.

Samuel Schoenbaum: *William Shakespeare: A Compact Documentary Life* [1977]. Revised edition: New York and Oxford: Oxford University Press, 1987.

The Woman's Part: Feminist Criticism of Shakespeare, ed. C. R. S. Lenz, G. Greene and C. T. Neely. Urbana, Ill.: University of Illinois Press, 1980.

Coppélia Kahn: *Man's Estate: Masculine Identity in Shakespeare*. Berkeley: University of California Press, 1981.

Lisa Jardine: *Still Harping on Daughters: Women and Drama in the Age of Shakespeare*. Brighton: Harvester, 1983.

Marianne Novy: *Love's Argument: Gender Relations in Shakespeare*. Chapel Hill and London: University of North Carolina Press, 1984.

Tori Haring-Smith: *From Farce to Metadrama: A Stage History of 'The Taming of the Shrew', 1594–1983*. Westport, Conn.: Greenwood Press, 1985.

'Bad' Shakespeare: Revaluations of the Shakespeare Canon, ed. Maurice Charney. Cranbury, N.J.: Associated University Presses, 1988.

Graham Holderness: Shakespeare in Performance: The Taming of the Shrew. Manchester: Manchester University Press, 1989.

Shakespeare: Early Comedies: A Casebook, ed. Pamela Mason. Basingstoke and London: Macmillan, 1995.

Russ McDonald: The Bedford Companion to Shakespeare: An Introduction with Documents. Basingstoke: Macmillan, 1996.

William Empson: The Strengths of Shakespeare's Shrew: Essays, Memoirs and Reviews. Sheffield: Sheffield Academic Press, 1996.

Daniel Rosenthal: Shakespeare on Screen. London: Hamlyn, 2000.

Sara Werner: Shakespeare and Feminist Performance: Ideology on Stage. London: Routledge, 2001.

The Taming of the Shrew: Critical Essays and Theatre Reviews, ed. Diana E. Espinall. London: Routledge, 2001.

The Cambridge Companion to Shakespearean Comedy, ed. Alexander Leggatt. Cambridge: Cambridge University Press, 2002.

NOTE ON SHAKESPEARE

William Shakespeare was the son of a glover at Stratford-upon-Avon, and tradition gives his date of birth as 23 April, 1564; certainly, three days later, he was christened at the parish church. It is likely that he attended the local Grammar School but had no university education. Of his early career there is no record, though John Aubrey reports a claim that he was a rural schoolmaster. In 1582 Shakespeare married Anne Hathaway, with whom he had two daughters, Susanna and Judith, and a son, Hamnet, who died in 1596. How he became involved with the stage in London is uncertain, but by 1592 he was sufficiently established as a playwright to be criticised in print as a challengingly versatile 'upstart Crow'. He was a leading member of the Lord Chamberlain's company, which became the King's Men on the accession of James I in 1603. Being not only a playwright and actor but also a 'sharer' (one of the owners of the company, entitled to a share of the profits), Shakespeare prospered greatly, as is proven by the numerous records of his financial transactions. Towards the end of his life, he loosened his ties with London and retired to New Place, the large house in Stratford-upon-Avon which he had bought in 1597. He died on 23 April, 1616, and is buried in the place of his baptism, Holy Trinity Church. The earliest collected edition of his plays, the First Folio, was published in 1623, and its prefatory verse-tributes include Ben Jonson's famous declaration, 'He was not of an age, but for all time'.

ACKNOWLEDGEMENTS AND TEXTUAL MATTERS

I have consulted – and am indebted to – numerous editions of *The Taming of the Shrew*, notably those by: Sir Arthur Quiller-Couch and John Dover Wilson ('The New Shakespeare': London: Cambridge University Press, 1928; revised and reprinted, 1953 and 1962; revised and abridged as 'The Cambridge Pocket Shakespeare', 1965); Peter Alexander (London and Glasgow: Collins, 1951; rpt. 1966); G. R. Hibbard ('The New Penguin Shakespeare': Harmondsworth: Penguin, 1968); G. Blakemore Evans *et al.* (*The Riverside Shakespeare*: Boston, Mass.: Houghton Mifflin, 1974); Brian Morris ('The Arden Shakespeare': London and New York: Methuen, 1981); H. J. Oliver ('The Oxford Shakespeare': Oxford: Oxford University Press, 1982); Stanley Wells and Gary Taylor (*The Complete Works*: Oxford: Oxford University Press, 1986); Ann Thompson (the 'New Cambridge Shakespeare': Cambridge: Cambridge University Press, 1984); and Stephen Greenblatt *et al.* (*The Norton Shakespeare*: New York and London: Norton, 1997). Fausto Cercignani's *Shakespeare's Works and Elizabethan Pronunciation* (Oxford: Oxford University Press, 1981) proved helpful. Professor Mario Curreli, once again, patiently provided wise advice on various topics, notably the Italian phrases in the play.

I turn now to textual matters: they may seem dry at first, but you will soon see their importance. The terms 'quarto' and 'folio' crop up. A 'quarto' is a book with relatively small pages, while a 'folio' is a book with relatively large pages. A quarto volume is made of sheets of paper, each of which has been folded twice to form four leaves (and thus eight pages), whereas each of a folio's sheets has been folded once to form two leaves (and thus four pages). As was mentioned in the Introduction, *The Taming of the Shrew* is one of Shakespeare's earliest comedies: it was probably written in the period 1590–92. An anonymous play called *The Taming of a Shrew* was entered on the Stationers' Register on 2 May 1594 and was published in quarto form in the same year. Shakespeare's *The Taming of the Shrew* was first published in the First Folio of 1623, seven years after the playwright's death. That First Folio ('F1') was the original 'collected edition' of Shakespeare's plays, assembled by two of the fellow-actors in his company, John Heminge (or Heminges) and Henry Condell. In that collection, the text of *The Taming of the Shrew* may have been based on a transcript of Shakespeare's 'foul papers' (an untidy manuscript). Evidently, however, cuts were made in the material before the F1 text was printed; and the eventual printing contains numerous errors: notably, verse-lines rendered unmetrical by the omission of a short word (e.g., 'As before imparted to your worship' instead of 'As I before imparted to your worship'). Indeed, as was noted in the Introduction, many verse-lines are oddly lame or irregular, indicating careless transmission; and this perhaps included some rushed work by the transcriber or compositor or both. In 1632 appeared the Second Folio ('F2'), which made numerous small changes and corrections to the play, often restoring the metre of marred lines.

The relationship between the anonymous *The Taming of a Shrew* and Shakespeare's *The Taming of the Shrew* has long been a topic of scholarly debate. One view is that the anonymous work was the source of Shakespeare's play; another is that both it and Shakespeare's play derive independently from a lost earlier play on the 'Shrew' theme'; and the currently prevailing view is that the anonymous work is partly a rather-garbled recollection of Shakespeare's play as staged and partly a free adaptation of it (incorporating new material). The obvious text to provide the basis of any new edition of Shakespeare's *The Taming of the Shrew* is thus the First Folio version. A difficulty, however, is that in F1 the Christopher Sly material seems incomplete. It is like a picture-frame of which half has become lost. The drama of the deception of Sly leads into the main 'Shrew' play and is briefly resumed just before Petruchio's entry; and, logically, when the 'Shrew' play ends, we should next see the termination of the Sly drama; but that termination is lacking. *The Taming of a Shrew*, on the other hand, *does* contain the termination, in addition to some further intermediate Sly – there 'Slie' – material, all of which probably derives (in however debased or improvised a form) from the original Shakespearian play. Consequently, stage-productions of Shakespeare's *The Taming of the Shrew* have often borrowed that terminal matter, and sometimes borrowed that intermediate matter, from *The Taming of a Shrew*. There is evidence, for example, that some Sly material was cut from what is now the transition between Act 5, scene 1, and Act 5, scene 2. In this edition, I have therefore supplied, in an Appendix, the 'Slie' matter of the anonymous play. As is customary in modern editions of Shakespeare, I have variously modernised the spelling, punctuation and stage-directions of F1, and have followed suit in the case of the appended Slie text. In the notes, however, quotations from F1 are not modernised, so that the reader can infer the extent of such changes.

The Taming of the Shrew thus illustrates the general rule that a play by Shakespeare was initially a quantity of script-material which, in course of time, could be revised, adapted, perhaps cut, perhaps expanded, by the playwright himself but also by others, as occasion demanded. Far from being fixed and finalised, the matter was highly variable. Sometimes a play might be 'reported' and partly rewritten by actors. After Shakespeare's life-time, the process of adaptation and variation continued at the hands of editors, printers, directors, players and translators.

The present edition of *The Taming of the Shrew* offers a practical compromise between the F1 text, Shakespeare's intentions (insofar as they can be reasonably inferred) and modern requirements. In the interest of fidelity to Shakespeare's likely usages, I have retained certain archaisms which some other editions modernise: for instance, I have preserved the occasional use of 'and' to mean 'if' and of 'a' to mean 'he'. The glossary explains such archaisms and unfamiliar terms, while the annotations offer clarification of obscurities. No edition of the play can claim to be definitive, but this one – aiming at clarity and concise practicality – can promise to be very useful.

THE TAMING OF THE SHREW

CHARACTERS:
IN THE INDUCTION:

CHRISTOPHER SLY, *a tinker.*

HOSTESS.

LORD.

PAGE, HUNTSMEN, SERVANTS *and* MESSENGER,
    all attending the lord.

COMPANY OF PLAYERS.

IN THE MAIN PLAY:

BAPTISTA MINOLA, *a wealthy Paduan.*

KATHERINA (Kate), *Baptista's elder daughter.*

BIANCA, *Baptista's younger daughter.*

PETRUCHIO, *suitor to Katherina.*

GRUMIO, *Petruchio's personal servant.*

CURTIS, *chief servant at Petruchio's country house.*

NATHANIEL, PHILIP, JOSEPH, NICHOLAS *and* PETER, *other
    servants of Petruchio.*

GREMIO, *suitor to Bianca.*

HORTENSIO, *another suitor to Bianca.*

LUCENTIO, *yet another suitor to Bianca.*

TRANIO, *Lucentio's personal servant.*

PETER, *servant with Tranio.*

BIONDELLO, *boy-servant to Lucentio.*

VINCENTIO, *Lucentio's father.*

WIDOW.

PEDANT.

TAILOR *and* HABERDASHER.

OFFICER.

NAMELESS GUESTS, MINSTRELS, SERVANTS *and* ATTENDANTS.

THE TAMING OF THE SHREW[1]

THE INDUCTION, SCENE I.

Outside a rural tavern.

Enter, from the tavern, CHRISTOPHER SLY, *driven by the* HOSTESS.

SLY	I'll feeze you, in faith!
HOSTESS	A pair of stocks, you rogue!
SLY	Y'are a baggage; the Slys are no rogues. Look in the chronicles: we came in with Richard Conqueror;[2] therefore *paucas pallabris*, let the world slide. Sessa!
HOSTESS	You will not pay for the glasses you have burst?
SLY	No, not a denier. Go by, Saint Jeronimie;[3] go to thy cold bed, and warm thee.

                 [He lies down.

HOSTESS	I know my remedy: I must go fetch the thirdborough.

                       [Exit.

SLY	Third, or fourth, or fifth borough, I'll answer him by law.[4] I'll not budge an inch, boy; let him come, and kindly. *[He falls asleep.*	10

Hunting-horns sound. Enter a LORD *and his train of*
HUNTSMEN *and* SERVANTS.

LORD	Huntsman, I charge thee, tender well my hounds. Breathe Merriman – the poor cur is embossed – And couple Clowder with the deep-mouthed brach. Saw'st thou not, boy, how Silver made it good At the hedge corner, in the coldest fault?[5] I would not lose the dog for twenty pound.	
HUNT. I	Why, Belman is as good as he, my lord: He cried upon it at the merest loss, And twice today picked out the dullest scent. Trust me, I take him for the better dog.	20
LORD	Thou art a fool. If Echo were as fleet, I would esteem him worth a dozen such. But sup them well, and look unto them all: Tomorrow I intend to hunt again.	
HUNT. I	I will, my lord. *[They notice Sly.*	

LORD	What's here? One dead, or drunk? See, doth he breathe?
HUNT. 2	He breathes, my lord. Were he not warmed with ale,
	This were a bed but cold to sleep so soundly. 30
LORD	O monstrous beast! How like a swine he lies!
	Grim death, how foul and loathsome is thine image!
	– Sirs, I will practise on this drunken man.
	What think you: if he were conveyed to bed,
	Wrapped in sweet clothes, rings put upon his fingers,
	A most delicious banquet by his bed,
	And brave attendants near him when he wakes,
	Would not the beggar then forget himself?
HUNT. 1	Believe me, lord, I think he cannot choose.
HUNT. 2	It would seem strange unto him when he waked. 40
LORD	Even as a flatt'ring dream or worthless fancy.
	Then take him up, and manage well the jest:
	Carry him gently to my fairest chamber,
	And hang it round with all my wanton pictures;
	Balm his foul head in warm distillèd waters,
	And burn sweet wood to make the lodging sweet;
	Procure me music ready when he wakes,
	To make a dulcet and a heavenly sound;
	And if he chance to speak, be ready straight,
	And with a low submissive reverence 50
	Say 'What is it your Honour will command?'.
	Let one attend him with a silver basin
	Full of rose-water and bestrewed with flowers;
	Another bear the ewer; the third a diaper,
	And say 'Will't please your lordship cool your hands?'.
	Someone be ready with a costly suit,
	And ask him what apparel he will wear;
	Another tell him of his hounds and horse,
	And that his lady mourns at his disease;
	Persuade him that he hath been lunatic, 60
	And when he says he is,[6] say that he dreams,
	For he is nothing but a mighty lord.
	This do, and do it kindly, gentle sirs:
	It will be pastime passing excellent,
	If it be husbanded with modesty.
HUNT. 1	My lord, I warrant you we will play our part,

	As he shall think by our true diligence
	He is no less than what we say he is.
LORD	Take him up gently and to bed with him,
	And each one to his office when he wakes. 70

[Sly is carried off. A trumpet sounds.

Sirrah, go see what trumpet 'tis that sounds –

[Exit servant.

Belike some noble gentleman that means
(Travelling some journey) to repose him here.

Enter SERVANT.

How now? Who is it?

SERVANT	An't please your honour, players
	That offer service to your Lordship.
LORD	Bid them come near.

Enter PLAYERS.

Now, fellows, you are welcome.

PLAYERS	We thank your Honour.
LORD	Do you intend to stay with me tonight?
PLAYER I	So please your Lordship to accept our duty.
LORD	With all my heart. This fellow I remember, 80
	Since once he played a farmer's eldest son:
	'Twas where you wooed the gentlewoman so well.
	I have forgot your name; but, sure, that part
	Was aptly fitted and naturally performed.
PLAYER 2	I think 'twas Soto that your honour means.[7]
LORD	'Tis very true; thou didst it excellent.
	Well, you are come to me in happy time,
	The rather for I have some sport in hand
	Wherein your cunning can assist me much.
	There is a lord will hear you play tonight; 90
	But I am doubtful of your modesties,
	Lest, over-eyeing of his odd behaviour
	(For yet his honour never heard a play),
	You break into some merry passion,
	And so offend him: for I tell you, sirs,
	If you should smile, he grows impatient.[8]
PLAYER I	Fear not, my lord: we can contain ourselves,
	Were he the veriest antic in the world.

LORD   [*to servant:*] Go, sirrah, take them to the buttery,
And give them friendly welcome every one: 100
Let them want nothing that my house affords.
                [*Exeunt players, led by that servant.*
[*To servant:*] Sirrah, go you to Barthol'mew my page,
And see him dressed in all suits like a lady;
That done, conduct him to the drunkard's chamber,
And call him 'madam', do him obeisance.
Tell him from me, as he will win my love,
He bear himself with honourable action,
Such as he hath observed in noble ladies
Unto their lords, by them accomplishèd.
Such duty to the drunkard let him do,   110
With soft low tongue and lowly courtesy,
And say: 'What is't your Honour will command,
Wherein your lady and your humble wife
May show her duty and make known her love?'.
And then with kind embracements, tempting kisses,
And with declining head into his bosom,
Bid him shed tears, as being overjoyed
To see her noble lord restored to health,
Who for this seven years hath esteemed him
No better than a poor and loathsome beggar;   120
And if the boy have not a woman's gift
To rain a shower of commanded tears,
An onion will do well for such a shift,
Which in a napkin (being close conveyed)
Shall in despite enforce a watery eye.
See this dispatched with all the haste thou canst;
Anon I'll give thee more instructions.   [*Exit servant.*
I know the boy will well usurp the grace,
Voice, gait and action of a gentlewoman:
I long to hear him call the drunkard 'husband',   130
And how my men will stay themselves from laughter
When they do homage to this simple peasant.
I'll in to counsel them: haply my presence
May well abate the over-merry spleen,
Which otherwise would grow into extremes.
                          [*Exeunt.*

SCENE 2.

A room in the lord's house.

Enter, aloft, SLY, SERVANTS *(some with apparel, others with a basin, a ewer and other appurtenances) and the* LORD.[9]

SLY   For God's sake, a pot of small ale!

SERVANT I   Will't please your Lordship drink a cup of sack?

SERVANT 2   Will't please your Honour taste of these conserves?

SERVANT 3   What raiment will your Honour wear today?

SLY   I am Christophero Sly; call not me 'Honour' nor
'Lordship'. I ne'er drank sack in my life; and if you give
me any conserves, give me conserves of beef. Ne'er ask
me what raiment I'll wear, for I have no more doublets
than backs, no more stockings than legs, nor no more
shoes than feet – nay, sometime more feet than shoes,   10
or such shoes as my toes look through the over-leather.

LORD   Heaven cease this idle humour in your Honour!
O, that a mighty man, of such descent,
Of such possessions and so high esteem,
Should be infusèd with so foul a spirit!

SLY   What, would you make me mad? Am not I Christopher
Sly, old Sly's son of Burton-Heath, by birth a pedlar,
by education a card-maker, by transmutation a bear-
herd, and now by present profession a tinker? Ask
Marian Hacket, the fat ale-wife of Wincot, if she know   20
me not:[10] if she say I am not fourteen pence on the
score for sheer ale, score me up for the lying'st knave in
Christendom. What! I am not bestraught: here's –

SERVANT 3   O, this it is that makes your lady mourn.

SERVANT 2   O, this it is that makes your servants droop.

LORD   Hence comes it that your kindred shuns your house,
As beaten hence by your strange lunacy.
O, noble lord, bethink thee of thy birth,
Call home thy ancient thoughts from banishment,
And banish hence these abject lowly dreams.   30
Look how thy servants do attend on thee,
Each in his office ready at thy beck.

Wilt thou have music? Hark, Apollo plays,   [*Music.*
And twenty cagèd nightingales do sing.
Or wilt thou sleep? We'll have thee to a couch
Softer and sweeter than the lustful bed
On purpose trimmed up for Semiramis.[11]
Say thou wilt walk: we will bestrow the ground.
Or wilt thou ride? Thy horses shall be trapped,
Their harness studded all with gold and pearl.   40
Dost thou love hawking? Thou hast hawks will soar
Above the morning lark. Or wilt thou hunt?
Thy hounds shall make the welkin answer them,
And fetch shrill echoes from the hollow earth.

SERVANT 1 Say thou wilt course: thy greyhounds are as swift
As breathèd stags, ay, fleeter than the roe.

SERVANT 2 Dost thou love pictures? We will fetch thee straight
Adonis painted by a running brook,
And Cytherea all in sedges hid,
Which seem to move and wanton with her breath,   50
Even as the waving sedges play with wind.[12]

LORD   We'll show thee Io as she was a maid,
And how she was beguiled and surprised,
As lively painted as the deed was done.[13]

SERVANT 3 Or Daphne roaming through a thorny wood,
Scratching her legs that one shall swear she bleeds;
And at that sight shall sad Apollo weep,
So workmanly the blood and tears are drawn.[14]

LORD   Thou art a lord, and nothing but a lord.
Thou hast a lady far more beautiful   60
Than any woman in this waning age.[15]

SERVANT 1 And, till the tears that she hath shed for thee
Like envious floods o'er-run her lovely face,
She was the fairest creature in the world;
And yet she is inferior to none.

SLY   Am I a lord, and have I such a lady?
Or do I dream? Or have I dreamed till now?
I do not sleep: I see, I hear, I speak;
I smell sweet savours, and I feel soft things:
Upon my life, I am a lord indeed,   70
And not a tinker, nor Christopher Sly.

Well, bring our lady hither to our sight,
And once again a pot o'th'smallest ale.

SERVANT 2 Will't please your Mightiness to wash your hands?

[*Sly washes.*

O, how we joy to see your wit restored!
O, that once more you knew but what you are!
These fifteen years you have been in a dream,
Or, when you waked, so waked as if you slept.

SLY 'These fifteen years'! By my fay, a goodly nap.
But did I never speak of all that time?   80

SERVANT 1 O, yes, my lord, but very idle words,
For though you lay here in this goodly chamber,
Yet would you say ye were beaten out of door,
And rail upon the hostess of the house,
And say you would present her at the leet
Because she brought stone jugs and no sealed quarts.[16]
Sometimes, you would call out for Cicely Hacket.

SLY Ay, the woman's maid of the house.

SERVANT 3 Why, sir, you know no house, nor no such maid,
Nor no such men as you have reckoned up,   90
As Stephen Sly, and old John Naps of Greece,[17]
And Peter Turph, and Henry Pimpernell,
And twenty more such names and men as these,
Which never were, nor no man ever saw.

SLY Now, Lord be thankèd for my good amends!

ALL Amen.

Enter the PAGE *(Bartholomew), dressed as a lady, and* ATTENDANTS
(one of whom gives Sly a pot of ale).

SLY   I thank thee; thou shalt not lose by it.

PAGE How fares my noble lord?

SLY   Marry, I fare well,
For here is cheer enough. [*He drinks.*] Where is my wife?

PAGE Here, noble lord; what is thy will with her?

SLY Are you my wife, and will not call me 'husband'?   100
My men should call me 'lord'; I am your good-man.

PAGE My husband and my lord, my lord and husband,
I am your wife in all obedience.

SLY I know it well. – What must I call her?

LORD   'Madam'.

SLY   'Al'ce madam', or 'Joan madam'?

LORD   'Madam' and nothing else: so lords call ladies.

SLY   — Madam wife, they say that I have dreamed
         And slept above some fifteen year or more.

PAGE   Ay, and the time seems thirty unto me,
         Being all this time abandoned from your bed.   110

SLY   'Tis much. Servants, leave me and her alone.
                                    [*Exeunt the servants.*
         Madam, undress you and come now to bed.

PAGE   Thrice-noble lord, let me entreat of you
         To pardon me yet for a night or two;
         Or, if not so, until the sun be set:
         For your physicians have expressly charged,
         In peril to incur your former malady,
         That I should yet absent me from your bed.
         I hope this reason stands for my excuse.

SLY   Ay, it stands so that I may hardly tarry so long;[18] but 120
         I would be loath to fall into my dreams again: I will
         therefore tarry in despite of the flesh and the blood.

                        Enter MESSENGER.

MESSEN. Your Honour's players, hearing your amendment,
         Are come to play a pleasant comedy;
         For so your doctors hold it very meet,
         Seeing too much sadness hath congealed your blood,
         And melancholy is the nurse of frenzy:
         Therefore they thought it good you hear a play[19]
         And frame your mind to mirth and merriment,
         Which bars a thousand harms and lengthens life.   130

SLY   Marry, I will let them play it. Is not a comonty
         A Christmas gambold or a tumbling-trick?

PAGE   No, my good lord, it is more pleasing stuff.

SLY   What, household stuff?

PAGE   It is a kind of history.

SLY   Well, we'll see't.   [*Exit messenger.*
                        Come, madam wife, sit by my side
         And let the world slip: we shall ne'er be younger.
                                    [*The page sits beside him.*

         A flourish of trumpets sounds to herald the impending play.

THE TAMING OF THE SHREW, ACT I, SCENE I.

A street in Padua.

Enter LUCENTIO *and his servant* TRANIO.

LUCENTIO   Tranio, since for the great desire I had
    To see fair Padua, nursery of arts,
    I am arrived for fruitful Lombardy,
    The pleasant garden of great Italy,
    And by my father's love and leave am armed
    With his good will and thy good company,
    My trusty servant well approved in all,
    Here let us breathe and haply institute
    A course of learning and ingenious studies.
    Pisa, renownèd for grave citizens,   10
    Gave me my being and my father first,
    A merchant of great traffic through the world,
    Vincentio, come of the Bentivolii.
    Vincentio's son, brought up in Florence,
    It shall become to serve all hopes conceived,
    To deck his fortune with his virtuous deeds;
    And therefore, Tranio, for the time I study
    Virtue, and that part of philosophy
    Will I apply that treats of happiness
    By virtue specially to be achieved.   20
    Tell me thy mind, for I have Pisa left
    And am to Padua come as he that leaves
    A shallow plash to plunge him in the deep,
    And with saciety seeks to quench his thirst.

TRANIO   *Perdonatemi*,[20] gentle master mine:
    I am in all affected as yourself,
    Glad that you thus continue your resolve
    To suck the sweets of sweet philosophy.
    Only, good master, while we do admire
    This virtue and this moral discipline,   30
    Let's be no Stoics nor no stocks, I pray,
    Or so devote to Aristotle's checks

As Ovid be an outcast quite abjured.[21]
Balk logic with acquaintance that you have,
And practise rhetoric in your common talk;
Music and poesy use to quicken you;
The mathematics and the metaphysics,
Fall to them as you find your stomach serves you:
No profit grows where is no pleasure tane.
In brief, sir, study what you most affect.   40

LUCENTIO Gramercies, Tranio, well dost thou advise.
If, Biondello, thou wert come ashore,
We could at once put us in readiness,
And take a lodging fit to entertain
Such friends as time in Padua shall beget.
But stay awhile, what company is this?

TRANIO   Master, some show to welcome us to town.
                          [*Lucentio and Tranio stand aside.*

Enter BAPTISTA *with* KATHERINA *and* BIANCA *(his daughters),*
    GREMIO *(a pantaloon) and* HORTENSIO *(suitor to Bianca).*

BAPTISTA Gentlemen, impórtune me no farther,
For how I firmly am resolved you know:
That is, not to bestow my youngest daughter   50
Before I have a husband for the elder.
If either of you both love Katherina,
Because I know you well, and love you well,
Leave shall you have to court her at your pleasure.

GREMIO   To *cart* her, rather: she's too rough for me.
– There, there, Hortensio, will you any wife?

KATHERINA [*to Baptista:*] I pray you, sir, is it your will
To make a stale of me amongst these mates?[23]

HORTENSIO 'Mates', maid? How mean you that? No mates for you,
Unless you were of gentler, milder mould.   60

KATHERINA I'faith, sir, you shall never need to fear.
Iwis, it is not half-way to her heart;[24]
But if it were, doubt not her care should be
To comb your noddle with a three-legged stool,
And paint your face, and use you like a fool.

HORTENSIO From all such devils, good Lord deliver us![25]

GREMIO   And me too, good Lord!

TRANIO   Husht, master! Here's some good pastime tóward;
            That wench is stark mad, or wonderful fróward.

LUCENTIO   But in the other's silence do I see   70
            Maid's mild behaviour and sobriety.
            Peace, Tranio.

TRANIO   Well said, master; mum, and gaze your fill.

BAPTISTA   Gentlemen, that I may soon make good
            What I have said – Bianca, get you in;
            And let it not displease thee, good Bianca,
            For I will love thee ne'er the less, my girl.

KATHERINA   A pretty peat! It is best
            Put finger in the eye, and she knew why.[26]

BIANCA   Sister, content you in my discontent.   80
            – Sir, to your pleasure humbly I subscribe:
            My books and instruments shall be my company,
            On them to look and practise by myself.

LUCENTIO   Hark, Tranio! Thou mayst hear Minerva speak.

HORTENSIO   Signor Baptista,[27] will you be so strange?
            Sorry am I that our good will effects
            Bianca's grief.

GREMIO   Why will you mew her up,
            Signor Baptista, for this fiend of hell,
            And make her bear the penance of her tongue?

BAPTISTA   Gentlemen, content ye; I am resolved.   90
            – Go in, Bianca. –   [Exit Bianca.
            And for I know she taketh most delight
            In music, instruments, and poetry,
            Schoolmasters will I keep within my house,
            Fit to instruct her youth. If you, Hortensio,
            Or Signor Gremio, you, know any such,
            Prefer them hither: for, to cunning men
            I will be very kind, and liberal
            To mine own children in good bringing-up.
            And so farewell. – Katherina, you may stay,   100
            For I have more to cómmune with Bianca.   [Exit.

KATHERINA   Why, and I trust I may go too, may I not?
            What, shall I be appointed hours, as though, belike,
            I knew not what to take and what to leave? Ha![28]
                                              [She walks away.

GREMIO   You may go to the devil's dam: your gifts are so good, there's none will hold you. [*Exit Katherina.*
Their love is not so great, Hortensio, but we may blow our nails together, and fast it fairly out. Our cake's dough on both sides.[29] Farewell. Yet, for the love I bear my sweet Bianca, if I can by any means light on a fit man to teach her that wherein she delights, I will wish him to her father.

HORTENSIO So will I, Signor Gremio; but a word, I pray. Though the nature of our quarrel yet never brooked parle, know now, upon advice, it toucheth us both — that we may yet again have access to our fair mistress and be happy rivals in Bianca's love — to labour and effect one thing specially.

GREMIO   What's that, I pray?

HORTENSIO Marry, sir, to get a husband for her sister.

GREMIO   A husband? A devil.

HORTENSIO I say, a husband.

GREMIO   I say, a devil. Think'st thou, Hortensio, though her father be very rich, any man is so very a fool to be married to hell?

HORTENSIO Tush, Gremio: though it pass your patience and mine to endure her loud alarums, why, man, there be good fellows in the world, and a man could light on them, would take her with all faults, and money enough.

GREMIO   I cannot tell; but I had as lief take her dowry with this condition: to be whipped at the high cross every morning.

HORTENSIO Faith, as you say, there's small choice in rotten apples; but come, since this bar in law makes us friends, it shall be so far forth friendly maintained till, by helping Baptista's eldest daughter to a husband, we set his youngest free for a husband, and then have to't afresh. Sweet Bianca! Happy man be his dole. He that runs fastest gets the ring.[30] How say you, Signor Gremio?

GREMIO   I am agreed, and would I had given him the best horse in Padua to begin his wooing that would thoroughly woo her, wed her and bed her, and rid the house of her! Come on. [*Exeunt Gremio and Hortensio.*

TRANIO   I pray, sir, tell me, is it possible
           That love should of a sudden take such hold?
LUCENTIO   O Tranio, till I found it to be true,
           I never thought it possible or likely;
           But see, while idly I stood looking on,
           I found the effect of love-in-idleness,
           And now in plainness do confess to thee,   150
           That art to me as secret and as dear
           As Anna to the Queen of Carthage was:[31]
           Tranio, I burn, I pine, I perish, Tranio,
           If I achieve not this young modest girl.
           Counsel me, Tranio, for I know thou canst;
           Assist me, Tranio, for I know thou wilt.[32]
TRANIO   Master, it is no time to chide you now;
           Affection is not rated from the heart.
           If love have touched you, nought remains but so:
           '*Redime te captum quam queas minimo.*'[33]   160
LUCENTIO   Gramercies, lad. Go forward, this contents.
           The rest will comfort, for thy counsel's sound.
TRANIO   Master, you looked so longly on the maid,
           Perhaps you marked not what's the pith of all.
LUCENTIO   O yes, I saw sweet beauty in her face,
           Such as the daughter of Agenor had,
           That made great Jove to humble him to her hand,
           When with his knees he kissed the Cretan strand.[34]
TRANIO   Saw you no more? Marked you not how her sister
           Began to scold and raise up such a storm   170
           That mortal ears might hardly endure the din?
LUCENTIO   Tranio, I saw her coral lips to move,
           And with her breath she did perfúme the air.
           Sacred and sweet was all I saw in her.
TRANIO   [*aside:*] Nay, then 'tis time to stir him from his trance.
           [*Aloud:*] I pray, awake, sir: if you love the maid,
           Bend thoughts and wits to achieve her. Thus it stands:
           Her elder sister is so curst and shrewd
           That till the father rid his hands of her,
           Master, your love must live a maid at home;   180
           And therefore has he closely mewed her up,
           Because she will not be annoyed with suitors.[35]

LUCENTIO Ah, Tranio, what a cruel father's he!
          But art thou not advised, he took some care
          To get her cunning schoolmasters to instruct her?
TRANIO   Ay, marry, am I, sir – and now 'tis plotted!
LUCENTIO I have it, Tranio!
TRANIO   Master, for my hand,
          Both our inventions meet and jump in one.
LUCENTIO Tell me thine first.
TRANIO   You will be schoolmaster,
          And undertake the teaching of the maid: 19
          That's your device.
LUCENTIO   It is: may it be done?
TRANIO   Not possible; for who shall bear your part,
          And be in Padua here Vincentio's son,
          Keep house and ply his book, welcome his friends,
          Visit his countrymen and banquet them?
LUCENTIO *Basta*! Content thee, for I have it full.
          We have not yet been seen in any house,
          Nor can we be distinguished by our faces
          For man or master. Then it follows thus:
          Thou shalt be master, Tranio, in my stead;   20
          Keep house and port and servants, as I should;
          I will some other be, some Florentine,
          Some Neapolitan, or meaner man of Pisa.
          'Tis hatched, and shall be so: Tranio, at once
          Uncase thee; take my coloured hat and cloak.
          When Biondello comes, he waits on thee,
          But I will charm him first to keep his tongue.
TRANIO   So had you need.   [*They exchange outfits.*
          In brief, sir, sith it your pleasure is,
          And I am tied to be obedient   21
          (For so your father charged me at our parting:
          'Be serviceable to my son', quoth he;
          Although I think 'twas in another sense),
          I am content to be Lucentio,
          Because so well I love Lucentio.
LUCENTIO Tranio, be so, because Lucentio loves;
          And let me be a slave, t'achieve that maid
          Whose sudden sight hath thralled my wounded eye.

Enter BIONDELLO.

           Here comes the rogue. – Sirrah, where have you been?
BIONDELLO Where have I been? Nay, how now, where are *you*?   220
           Master, has my fellow Tranio stol'n your clothes,
           Or you stol'n his, or both? Pray, what's the news?[36]
LUCENTIO Sirrah, come hither. 'Tis no time to jest,
           And therefore frame your manners to the time.
           Your fellow Tranio here, to save my life,
           Puts my apparel and my count'nance on,
           And I for my escape have put on his;
           For, in a quarrel since I came ashore,
           I killed a man, and fear I was descried.
           Wait you on him, I charge you, as becomes,   230
           While I make way from hence to save my life:
           You understand me?
BIONDELLO   I sir? Ne'er a whit.[37]
LUCENTIO And not a jot of 'Tranio' in your mouth.
           Tranio is changed into Lucentio.
BIONDELLO The better for him; would I were so too!
TRANIO   So could I, faith, boy, to have the next wish after,
           That Lucentio indeed had Baptista's youngest daughter.
           But, sirrah, not for my sake but your master's, I advise
           You use your manners discreetly in all kind of
                              companies:
           When I am alone, why, then I am Tranio;   240
           But in all places else, your master Lucentio.
LUCENTIO Tranio, let's go.
           One thing more rests, that thyself execute:
           To make one among these wooers. If thou ask me why,
           Sufficeth my reasons are both good and weighty.
                                [*Exeunt.*

The OBSERVERS *above speak.*[38]

SERVANT I My lord, you nod; you do not mind the play.
SLY   Yes, by Saint Anne, do I. A good matter, surely. Comes
           there any more of it?
PAGE   My lord, 'tis but begun.
SLY   'Tis a very excellent piece of work, madam lady.   250
           Would 'twere done!
                  [*They remain seated and observe.*[39]

SCENE 2.

A street in Padua, outside Hortensio's house.

Enter PETRUCHIO[40] *and his servant* GRUMIO.

PETRUCHIO Verona, for a while I take my leave
To see my friends in Padua, but of all
My best belovèd and approvèd friend,
Hortensio; and I trow this is his house.
– Here, sirrah Grumio, knock, I say.

GRUMIO Knock, sir? Whom should I knock? Is there any man
has rebused your worship?

PETRUCHIO Villain, I say, knock me here soundly.[41]

GRUMIO Knock you here, sir? Why, sir, what am I, sir, that I
should knock you here, sir?   10

PETRUCHIO Villain, I say, knock me at this gate,
And rap me well, or I'll knock your knave's pate.

GRUMIO My master is grown quarrelsome: I should knock
                                                you first,
And then I know after who comes by the worst.

PETRUCHIO Will it not be?
Faith, sirrah, and you'll not knock, I'll ring it!
I'll try how you can *sol-fa* and sing it.
                [*He wrings Grumio's ears, forcing him down.*[42]

GRUMIO Help, masters, help![43] My master is mad.

PETRUCHIO Now, knock when I bid you, sirrah villain!

Enter HORTENSIO *from the house.*

HORTENSIO How now, what's the matter? My old friend Grumio   20
and my good friend Petruchio! How do you all at
Verona?

PETRUCHIO Signor Hortensio, come you to part the fray?
Con tutto il cuore, ben trovato, may I say.

HORTENSIO *Alla nostra casa ben venuto, molto onorato signor mio
Petruccio.*[44]
Rise, Grumio, rise; we will compound this quarrel.

GRUMIO Nay, 'tis no matter, sir, what he 'leges in Latin. If this be
not a lawful cause for me to leave his service, look you,

         sir: he bid me knock him and rap him soundly, sir.   30
         Well, was it fit for a servant to use his master so, being
         perhaps (for aught I see) two-and-thirty, a pip out?[45]
         Whom would to God I had well knocked at first,
         Then had not Grumio come by the worst.

PETRUCHIO A senseless villain! Good Hortensio,
         I bade the rascal knock upon your gate,
         And could not get him for my heart to do it.

GRUMIO   Knock at the gate? O heavens! Spake you not these
         words plain, 'Sirrah, knock me here', 'rap me here',
         'knock me well', and 'knock me soundly'? And come   40
         you now with 'knocking at the gate'?

PETRUCHIO Sirrah, be gone, or talk not, I advise you.

HORTENSIO Petruchio, patience: I am Grumio's pledge.
         Why, this's a heavy chance 'twixt him and you,
         Your ancient, trusty, pleasant servant Grumio.
         And tell me now, sweet friend, what happy gale
         Blows you to Padua here from old Verona?

PETRUCHIO Such wind as scatters young men through the world,
         To seek their fortunes farther than at home,
         Where small experience grows but in a few.[46]   50
         Signor Hortensio, thus it stands with me:
         Antonio, my father, is deceased,
         And I have thrust myself into this maze,
         Happily to wive and thrive as best I may.
         Crowns in my purse I have, and goods at home,
         And so am come abroad to see the world.

HORTENSIO Petruchio, shall I then come roundly to thee,
         And wish thee to a shrewd ill-favoured wife?
         Thou'dst thank me but a little for my counsel;
         And yet I'll promise thee she shall be rich,   60
         And very rich; but th'art too much my friend,
         And I'll not wish thee to her.

PETRUCHIO Signor Hortensio, 'twixt such friends as we,
         Few words suffice; and therefore, if thou know
         One rich enough to be Petruchio's wife
         (As wealth is burthen of my wooing dance),
         Be she as foul as was Florentius' love,
         As old as Sibyl, and as curst and shrewd

As Socrates' Zentippe or a worse,
She moves me not, or not removes, at least,   70
Affection's edge in me, were she as rough[47]
As are the swelling Adriatic seas.
I come to wive it wealthily in Padua;
If wealthily, then happily in Padua.

GRUMIO   [to Hortensio:] Nay, look you, sir, he tells you flatly what
his mind is: why, give him gold enough, and marry him
to a puppet or an aglet-baby, or an old trot with ne'er a
tooth in her head, though she have as many diseases as
two-and-fifty horses: why, nothing comes amiss, so
money comes withal.   80

HORTENSIO Petruchio, since we are stepped thus far in,
I will continue that I broached in jest.
I can, Petruchio, help thee to a wife
With wealth enough, and young and beauteous,
Brought up as best becomes a gentlewoman.
Her only fault, and that is faults enough,
Is that she is intolerable curst
And shrewd and fróward, so beyond all measure,
That, were my state far worser than it is,
I would not wed her for a mine of gold.   90

PETRUCHIO Hortensio, peace; thou know'st not gold's effect.
Tell me her father's name, and 'tis enough;
For I will board her, though she chide as loud
As thunder when the clouds in autumn crack.

HORTENSIO Her father is Baptista Minola,
An affable and courteous gentleman;
Her name is Katherina Minola,
Renowned in Padua for her scolding tongue.

PETRUCHIO I know her father, though I know not her,
And he knew my deceasèd father well.   100
I will not sleep, Hortensio, till I see her,
And therefore let me be thus bold with you
To give you over at this first encounter,
Unless you will accompany me thither.

GRUMIO   [to Hortensio:] I pray you, sir, let him go while the
humour lasts. A'my word, and she knew him as well as
I do, she would think scolding would do little good

upon him. She may perhaps call him half a score knaves
or so: why, that's nothing; and he begin once, he'll rail
in his rope-tricks. I'll tell you what, sir: and she stand   110
him but a little, he will throw a figure in her face, and
so disfigure her with it, that she shall have no more eyes
to see withal than a cat.[48] You know him not, sir.

HORTENSIO Tarry, Petruchio; I must go with thee,
For in Baptista's keep my treasure is:
He hath the jewel of my life in hold,
His youngest daughter, beautiful Bianca,
And her withholds from me and other more,
Suitors to her and rivals in my love;
Supposing it a thing impossible,   120
For those defects I have before rehearsed,
That ever Katherina will be wooed;
Therefore this order hath Baptista tane,
That none shall have accéss unto Bianca
Till Katherine the curst have got a husband.

GRUMIO 'Katherine the curst'!
A title for a maid, of all titles the worst.

HORTENSIO Now shall my friend Petruchio do me grace,
And offer me, disguised in sober robes,
To old Baptista as a schoolmaster   130
Well seen in music, to instruct Bianca,
That so I may, by this device, at least
Have leave and leisure to make love to her,
And unsuspected court her by herself.

GRUMIO [aside:] Here's no knavery! See, to beguile the old
folks, how the young folks lay their heads together. –

Enter GREMIO, holding a reading-list, with LUCENTIO, who is disguised
as Cambio, a schoolmaster.[49]

Master, master, look about you! Who goes there, ha?

HORTENSIO Peace, Grumio; it is the rival of my love.
– Petruchio, stand by a while.

GRUMIO A proper stripling and an amorous!   [They stand aside. 140

GREMIO [to Lucentio:] O, very well; I have perused the note.
Hark you, sir, I'll have them very fairly bound –
All books of love, see that at any hand –
And see you read no other lectures to her:

You understand me. Over and beside
Signor Baptista's liberality,
I'll mend it with a largess. Take your paper too.
And let me have them very well perfúmed;
For she is sweeter than perfúme itself,
To whom they go. What will you read to her?⁵⁰   150

LUCENTIO Whate'er I read to her, I'll plead for you
As for my patron (stand you so assured
As firmly as yourself were still in place),
Yea, and perhaps with more successful words
Than you, unless you were a scholar, sir.

GREMIO O this learning, what a thing it is!

GRUMIO [aside:] O this woodcock, what an ass it is!

PETRUCHIO [aside:] Peace, sirrah.

HORTENSIO [aside:] Grumio, mum.
[He comes forward.]   God save you, Signor Gremio!

GREMIO And you are well met, Signor Hortensio.   160
Trow you whither I am going? To Baptista Minola.
I promised to inquire carefully
About a schoolmaster for the fair Bianca,
And by good fortune I have lighted well
On this young man, for learning and behaviour
Fit for her turn, well read in poetry
And other books – good ones, I warrant ye.

HORTENSIO 'Tis well; and I have met a gentleman
Hath promised me to help me to another,
A fine musician to instruct our mistress;   170
So shall I no whit be behind in duty
To fair Bianca, so beloved of me.

GREMIO Beloved of me, and that my deeds shall prove.

GRUMIO [aside:] And that his bags shall prove.

HORTENSIO Gremio, 'tis now no time to vent our love.
Listen to me, and if you speak me fair,
I'll tell you news indifferent good for either.
[He indicates Petruchio:] Here is a gentleman whom
                                        by chance I met,
Upon agreement from us to his liking,
Will undertake to woo curst Katherine,   180
Yea, and to marry her, if her dowry please.

GREMIO   So said, so done, is well.
            Hortensio, have you told him all her faults?

PETRUCHIO   I know she is an irksome brawling scold:
            If that be all, masters, I hear no harm.

GREMIO   No? Say'st me so, friend? What countryman?

PETRUCHIO   Born in Verona, old Antonio's son.
            My father dead, my fortune lives for me,[51]
            And I do hope good days and long to see.

GREMIO   O sir, such a life, with such a wife, were strange!   190
            But, if you have a stomach, to't a God's name;
            You shall have me assisting you in all.
            But will you woo this wild-cat?

PETRUCHIO   Will I live?

GRUMIO   [aside:] Will he woo her? Ay, or I'll hang her.[52]

PETRUCHIO   Why came I hither, but to that intent?
            Think you a little din can daunt mine ears?
            Have I not in my time heard lions roar?
            Have I not heard the sea, puffed up with winds,
            Rage like an angry boar chafèd with sweat?
            Have I not heard great ordnance in the field,   200
            And heaven's artillery thunder in the skies?
            Have I not in a pitchèd battle heard
            Loud 'larums, neighing steeds, and trumpets' clang?
            And do you tell me of a woman's tongue,
            That gives not half so great a blow to hear
            As will a chestnut in a farmer's fire?
            Tush, tush. Fear boys with bugs.

GRUMIO   [aside:]   For he fears none.

GREMIO   Hortensio, hark:
            This gentleman is happily arrived
            (My mind presumes) for his own good and yours.[53]   210

HORTENSIO   I promised we would be contributors
            And bear his charge of wooing, whatsoe'er.

GREMIO   And so we will, provided that he win her.

GRUMIO   I would I were as sure of a good dinner.

            Enter TRANIO *(disguised in fine clothing as Lucentio)*
                      and BIONDELLO.

TRANIO   Gentlemen, God save you! If I may be bold,
            Tell me, I beseech you, which is the readiest way

To the house of Signor Baptista Minola?

BIONDELLO He that has the two fair daughters: is't he you mean?

TRANIO Even he, Biondello.

GREMIO Hark you, sir! You mean not her to woo?   220

TRANIO Perhaps him and her, sir. What have you to do?

PETRUCHIO Not her that chides, sir, at any hand, I pray.[54]

TRANIO I love no chiders, sir. – Biondello, let's away.

LUCENTIO [aside:] Well begun, Tranio.

HORTENSIO   Sir, a word ere you go:
Are you a suitor to the maid you talk of, yea or no?

TRANIO And if I be, sir, is it any offence?

GREMIO No, if without more words you will get you hence.

TRANIO Why, sir, I pray, are not the streets as free
For me as for you?

GREMIO   But so is not she.

TRANIO For what reason, I beseech you?

GREMIO   For this reason, if you'll know,   230
That she's the choice love of Signor Gremio.

HORTENSIO That she's the chosen of Signor Hortensio!

TRANIO Softly, my masters! If you be gentlemen,
Do me this right: hear me with patience.
Baptista is a noble gentleman,
To whom my father is not all unknown,
And were his daughter fairer than she is,
She may more suitors have, and me for one.
Fair Leda's daughter had a thousand wooers,
Then well one more may fair Bianca have;   240
And so she shall: Lucentio shall make one,
Though Paris came in hope to speed alone.[55]

GREMIO What, this gentleman will out-talk us all!

LUCENTIO Sir, give him head; I know he'll prove a jade.

PETRUCHIO Hortensio, to what end are all these words?

HORTENSIO Sir, let me be so bold as ask you,
Did you yet ever see Baptista's daughter?

TRANIO No, sir, but hear I do that he hath two:
The one as famous for a scolding tongue
As is the other for beauteous modesty.   250

PETRUCHIO Sir, sir, the first's for me: let her go by.

GREMIO Yea, leave that labour to great Hercules,

And let it be more than Alcides' twelve.[56]

PETRUCHIO Sir, understand you this of me in sooth:
The youngest daughter, whom you hearken for,
Her father keeps from all accéss of suitors,
And will not promise her to any man
Until the elder sister first be wed.
The younger then is free, and not before.

TRANIO If it be so, sir, that you are the man   260
Must stead us all, and me amongst the rest,
And if you break the ice and do this feat,[57]
Achieve the elder, set the younger free
For our accéss: whose hap shall be to have her
Will not so graceless be to be ingrate.

HORTENSIO Sir, you say well, and well you do conceive;
And since you do profess to be a suitor,
You must, as we do, gratify this gentleman,
To whom we all rest generally beholding.

TRANIO Sir, I shall not be slack; in sign whereof,   260
Please ye we may convive this afternoon,
And quaff carouses to our mistress' health,
And do as adversaries do in law,
Strive mightily, but eat and drink as friends.

GRUMIO, BIONDELLO   O excellent motion! Fellows, let's be gone.

HORTENSIO The motion's good indeed, and be it so.
Petruchio, I shall be your *benvenuto*.[58]

                                                    [*Exeunt*.

ACT 2, SCENE 1.

Inside Baptista's house.

Enter BIANCA*, her clothing torn and her hands tied,*[59] *led by*
KATHERINA.

BIANCA	Good sister, wrong me not, nor wrong yourself,
	To make a bondmaid and a slave of me:
	That I disdain; but for these other goods,[60]
	Unbind my hands, I'll pull them off myself,
	Yea, all my raiment to my petticoat;
	Or what you will command me will I do,
	So well I know my duty to my elders.
KATHERINA	Of all thy suitors, here I charge thee, tell
	Whom thou lov'st best. See thou dissemble not.
BIANCA	Believe me, sister, of all the men alive 10
	I never yet beheld that special face
	Which I could fancy more than any other.
KATHERINA	Minion, thou liest! Is't not Hortensio?
BIANCA	If you affect him, sister, here I swear
	I'll plead for you myself, but you shall have him.
KATHERINA	O then, belike, you fancy riches more:
	You will have Gremio to keep you fair.
BIANCA	Is it for him you do envy me so?
	Nay, then you jest, and now I well perceive
	You have but jested with me all this while. 20
	I prithee, sister Kate, untie my hands.
KATHERINA	[*strikes her.*] If that be jest, then all the rest was so.

Enter BAPTISTA.

BAPTISTA	Why, how now, dame? Whence grows this insolence?
	– Bianca, stand aside. (Poor girl! she weeps.)

                                       [*He unties her hands.*

	Go ply thy needle, meddle not with her. –
	For shame, thou hilding of a devilish spirit,
	Why dost thou wrong her that did ne'er wrong thee?
	When did she cross thee with a bitter word?
KATHERINA	Her silence flouts me, and I'll be revenged.

                                       [*She rushes at Bianca.*

BAPTISTA   [*checks her.*] What, in my sight? – Bianca, get thee in.   30
                                              [*Exit Bianca.*

KATHERINA   What, will you not suffer me? Nay, now I see
            She is your treasure, she must have a husband;
            I must dance bare-foot on her wedding-day
            And, for your love to her, lead apes in hell.[61]
            Talk not to me; I will go sit and weep
            Till I can find occasion of revenge.   [*Exit.*

BAPTISTA   Was ever gentleman thus grieved as I?
            But who comes here?

Enter GREMIO, LUCENTIO *(dressed poorly, disguised as Cambio, the
schoolmaster),* PETRUCHIO, HORTENSIO *(disguised as Licio, the
musician), and* TRANIO *(disguised as Lucentio), with* BIONDELLO *(the
boy-servant, bearing a lute and books).*[62]

GREMIO   Good morrow, neighbour Baptista.

BAPTISTA   Good morrow, neighbour Gremio. God save you,   40
            gentlemen!

PETRUCHIO   And you, good sir. Pray, have you not a daughter
            Called Katherina, fair and virtuous?

BAPTISTA   I have a daughter, sir, called Katherina.

GREMIO   [*to Petruchio:*] You are too blunt; go to it orderly.

PETRUCHIO   You wrong me, Signor Gremio; give me leave.
            [*To Baptista:*] I am a gentleman of Verona, sir,
            That, hearing of her beauty and her wit,
            Her affability and bashful modesty,
            Her wondrous qualities and mild behaviour,   50
            Am bold to show myself a forward guest
            Within your house, to make mine eye the witness
            Of that report which I so oft have heard;
            And, for an entrance to my entertainment,
            I do present you with a man of mine,
                              [*He presents Hortensio.*
            Cunning in music and the mathematics,
            To instruct her fully in those sciences,
            Whereof I know she is not ignorant.
            Accept of him, or else you do me wrong.
            His name is Licio, born in Mantua.   60

BAPTISTA   Y'are welcome, sir, and he for your good sake;
            But, for my daughter Katherine, this I know:

She is not for your turn, the more my grief.

PETRUCHIO I see you do not mean to part with her,
Or else you like not of my company.

BAPTISTA Mistake me not, I speak but as I find.
Whence are you, sir? What may I call your name?

PETRUCHIO Petruchio is my name, Antonio's son,
A man well known throughout all Italy.

BAPTISTA I know him well: you are welcome for his sake.   70

GREMIO Saving your tale, Petruchio, I pray,
Let us, that are poor petitioners, speak too!
Backare! [63] You are marvellous forward.

PETRUCHIO O, pardon me, Signor Gremio: I would fain
                                        be doing.

GREMIO I doubt it not, sir; but you will curse your wooing.
[*To Baptista, indicating Hortensio:*] Neighbour, this is a
gift very grateful, I am sure of it. To express the like
kindness, myself, that have been more kindly beholding
to you than any, freely give unto you this young scholar,
[*He presents Lucentio.*] that hath been long studying at   80
Rheims, as cunning in Greek, Latin, and other languages,
as the other in music and mathematics. His name is
Cambio; pray accept his service.

BAPTISTA A thousand thanks, Signor Gremio; welcome, good
Cambio. [*He turns to Tranio:*] But, gentle sir, methinks
you walk like a stranger. May I be so bold to know the
cause of your coming?

TRANIO Pardon me, sir; the boldness is mine own,
That, being a stranger in this city here,
Do make myself a suitor to your daughter,   90
Unto Bianca, fair and virtuous;
Nor is your firm resolve unknown to me,
In the preferment of the eldest sister.
This liberty is all that I request:
That, upon knowledge of my parentage,
I may have welcome 'mongst the rest that woo,
And free accéss and favour as the rest.
And toward the education of your daughters
I here bestow a simple instrument,
And this small packet of Greek and Latin books.   100

                    [*Biondello comes forward with lute and books.*
            If you accept them, then their worth is great.
BAPTISTA   Lucentio is your name; of whence, I pray?
TRANIO   Of Pisa, sir, son to Vincentio.
BAPTISTA   A mighty man of Pisa; by report
            I know him well. You are very welcome, sir.
            [*To Hortensio:*]Take you the lute, [*to Lucentio:*] and you
                                        the set of books:
            You shall go see your pupils presently.
            Holla, within!

                        Enter a SERVANT.

                        Sirrah, lead these gentlemen
            To my daughters, and tell them both,
            These are their tutors; bid them use them well.   110
                    [*Exeunt servant, Hortensio and Lucentio.*
            We will go walk a little in the orchard,
            And then to dinner. You are passing welcome,
            And so I pray you all to think yourselves.
PETRUCHIO   Signor Baptista, my business asketh haste,
            And every day I cannot come to woo.
            You knew my father well, and in him me,
            Left solely heir to all his lands and goods,
            Which I have bettered rather than decreased.
            Then tell me: if I get your daughter's love,
            What dowry shall I have with her to wife?   120
BAPTISTA   After my death, the one half of my lands,
            And in possession twenty thousand crowns.
PETRUCHIO   And, for that dowry, I'll assure her of
            Her widowhood, be it that she survive me,
            In all my lands and leases whatsoever.
            Let specialties be therefore drawn between us,
            That covenants may be kept on either hand.
BAPTISTA   Ay, when the special thing is well obtained,
            That is, her love; for that is all in all.
PETRUCHIO   Why, that is nothing; for I tell you, father,   130
            I am as péremptory as she proud-minded;
            And where two raging fires meet together,
            They do consume the thing that feeds their fury.

Though little fire grows great with little wind,
Yet éxtreme gusts will blow out fire and all:
So I to her, and so she yields to me,
For I am rough and woo not like a babe.

BAPTISTA   Well mayst thou woo, and happy be thy speed;
But be thou armed for some unhappy words.

PETRUCHIO Ay, to the proof, as mountains are for winds,   140
That shakes not,[64] though they blow perpetually.

'Enter HORTENSIO *with his head broke.*'[65]

BAPTISTA   How now, my friend? Why dost thou look so pale?

HORTENSIO For fear, I promise you, if I look pale.

BAPTISTA   What, will my daughter prove a good musician?

HORTENSIO I think she'll sooner prove a soldier.
Iron may hold with her, but never lutes.

BAPTISTA   Why then, thou canst not break her to the lute?

HORTENSIO Why no, for she hath broke the lute to me.
I did but tell her she mistook her frets,[66]
And bowed her hand to teach her fingering,   150
When, with a most impatient devilish spirit,
'Frets, call you these?', quoth she, 'I'll fume with them!';
And, with that word, she struck me on the head,
And through the instrument my pate made way,
And there I stood amazèd for a while,
As on a pillory, looking through the lute,
While she did call me 'rascal fiddler'
And 'twangling Jack', with twenty such vilde terms,
As had she studied to misuse me so.

PETRUCHIO Now, by the world, it is a lusty wench!   160
I love her ten times more than e'er I did.
O, how I long to have some chat with her!

BAPTISTA   [*to Hortensio:*] Well, go with me, and be not so
                                        discomfited.
Proceed in practice with my younger daughter:
She's apt to learn, and thankful for good turns.
– Signor Petruchio, will you go with us,
Or shall I send my daughter Kate to you?

PETRUCHIO I pray you do. I'll attend her here –
                              [*Exeunt all except Petruchio.*

And woo her with some spirit when she comes.
Say that she rail, why then I'll tell her plain   170
She sings as sweetly as a nightingale;
Say that she frown, I'll say she looks as clear
As morning roses newly washed with dew;
Say she be mute and will not speak a word,
Then I'll commend her volubility,
And say she uttereth piercing eloquence.
If she do bid me pack, I'll give her thanks,
As though she bid me stay by her a week;
If she deny to wed, I'll crave the day
When I shall ask the banes, and when be married.   180
But here she comes, and now, Petruchio, speak.

Enter KATHERINA.

Good morrow, Kate, for that's your name, I hear.

KATHERINA Well have you heard, but something hard of hearing;
They call me 'Katherine' that do talk of me.

PETRUCHIO You lie, in faith, for you are called plain 'Kate',
And 'bonny Kate', and sometimes 'Kate the curst':
But Kate, the prettiest Kate in Christendom,
Kate of Kate Hall, my super-dainty Kate
(For dainties are all cates),[67] and therefore, Kate,
Take this of me, Kate of my consolation: 190
Hearing thy mildness praised in every town,
Thy virtues spoke of, and thy beauty sounded
(Yet not so deeply as to thee belongs),
Myself am moved to woo thee for my wife.

KATHERINA 'Moved', in good time! Let him that moved you hither
Remove you hence: I knew you at the first
You were a movable.[68]

PETRUCHIO   Why, what's a movable?

KATHERINA A joint-stool.

PETRUCHIO   Thou hast hit it: come, sit on me.

KATHERINA Asses are made to bear, and so are you.

PETRUCHIO Women are made to bear, and so are you.   200

KATHERINA No such jade as you, if me you mean.

PETRUCHIO Alas, good Kate, I will not burthen thee,
For, knowing thee to be but young and light, –

KATHERINA Too light for such a swain as you to catch,
          And yet as heavy as my weight should be.

PETRUCHIO 'Should be', should buzz!

KATHERINA   Well tane, and like a buzzard.

PETRUCHIO O, slow-winged turtle, shall a buzzard take thee?

KATHERINA Ay, for a turtle, as he takes a buzzard.[69]

PETRUCHIO Come, come, you wasp; i'faith, you are too angry.

KATHERINA If I be waspish, best beware my sting.   210

PETRUCHIO My remedy is then to pluck it out.

KATHERINA Ay, if the fool could find it where it lies.

PETRUCHIO Who knows not where a wasp doth wear his sting?
          In his tail.

KATHERINA   In his tongue.

PETRUCHIO   Whose tongue?

KATHERINA Yours, if you talk of tales, and so farewell.

                                        [*She turns to go.*

PETRUCHIO What, with my tongue in your tail? Nay, come again.

                                        [*He seizes her in his arms.*[70]

          Good Kate, I am a gentleman –

KATHERINA   That I'll try.

                                        [*She strikes him.*

PETRUCHIO I swear I'll cuff you, if you strike again.

KATHERINA So may you lose your arms.
          If you strike me, you are no gentleman,   220
          And if no gentleman, why then no arms.

PETRUCHIO A herald, Kate? O, put me in thy books![71]

KATHERINA What is your crest? A coxcomb?

PETRUCHIO A combless cock, so Kate will be my hen.

KATHERINA No cock of mine: you crow too like a craven.

PETRUCHIO Nay, come, Kate, come; you must not look so sour.

KATHERINA It is my fashion, when I see a crab.[72]

PETRUCHIO Why, here's no crab, and therefore look not sour.

KATHERINA There is, there is.

PETRUCHIO Then show it me.

KATHERINA   Had I a glass, I would.   230

PETRUCHIO What, you mean my face?

KATHERINA   Well aimed of such a young one.

PETRUCHIO Now, by Saint George, I am too young for you.

KATHERINA Yet you are withered.

PETRUCHIO   'Tis with cares.

KATHERINA   I care not.

PETRUCHIO Nay, hear you, Kate. In sooth, you scape not so.

KATHERINA I chafe you, if I tarry. Let me go!   [*She struggles.*

PETRUCHIO No, not a whit; I find you passing gentle.
       'Twas told me you were rough and coy and sullen,
       And now I find report a very liar,
       For thou art pleasant, gamesome, passing courteous,
       But slow in speech, yet sweet as spring-time flowers.   240
       Thou canst not frown, thou canst not look askance,
       Nor bite the lip, as angry wenches will,
       Nor hast thou pleasure to be cross in talk;
       But thou with mildness entertain'st thy wooers,
       With gentle conference, soft and affable.
                       [*He releases her.*
       Why does the world report that Kate doth limp?
       O sland'rous world! Kate like the hazel-twig
       Is straight and slender, and as brown in hue
       As hazel-nuts, and sweeter than the kernels.
       O, let me see thee walk: thou dost not halt.   250

KATHERINA Go, fool, and whom thou keep'st command!

PETRUCHIO Did ever Dian so become a grove
       As Kate this chamber with her princely gait?
       O, be thou Dian and let her be Kate,
       And then let Kate be chaste and Dian sportful![73]

KATHERINA Where did you study all this goodly speech?

PETRUCHIO It is extempore, from my mother-wit.

KATHERINA A witty mother; witless else her son.

PETRUCHIO Am I not wise?

KATHERINA   Yes, keep you warm.[74]

PETRUCHIO Marry, so I mean, sweet Katherine, in thy bed;   260
       And therefore, setting all this chat aside,
       Thus in plain terms: your father hath consented
       That you shall be my wife; your dowry 'greed on;
       And, will you, nill you, I will marry you.
       Now, Kate, I am a husband for your turn,
       For by this light whereby I see thy beauty
       (Thy beauty that doth make me like thee well),
       Thou must be married to no man but me,

For I am he am born to tame you, Kate,
And bring you from a wild Kate to a Kate   270
Conformable as other household Kates.[75]

Enter BAPTISTA, GREMIO *and* TRANIO *(as Lucentio).*

Here comes your father; never make denial:
I must and will have Katherine to my wife.

BAPTISTA   Now, Signor Petruchio, how speed you with
                                          my daughter?

PETRUCHIO   How but well, sir? How but well?
It were impossible I should speed amiss.

BAPTISTA   Why, how now, daughter Katherine? In your dumps?

KATHERINA   Call you me 'daughter'? Now I promise you,
You have showed a tender fatherly regard,
To wish me wed to one half-lunatic,   280
A mad-cap ruffian and a swearing Jack,
That thinks with oaths to face the matter out.

PETRUCHIO   Father, 'tis thus: yourself and all the world,
That talked of her, have talked amiss of her.
If she be curst, it is for policy,
For she's not fróward, but modest as the dove;
She is not hot, but temperate as the morn;
For patience she will prove a second Grissell,
And Roman Lucrece for her chastity;[76]
And to conclude, we have 'greed so well together,   290
That upon Sunday is the wedding-day.

KATHERINA   I'll see thee hanged on Sunday first!

GREMIO   Hark, Petruchio, she says she'll see thee hanged first.

TRANIO   Is this your speeding? Nay, then, good-night our part!

PETRUCHIO   Be patient, gentlemen. I choose her for myself.
If she and I be pleased, what's that to you?
'Tis bargained 'twixt us twain, being alone,
That she shall still be curst in company.
I tell you, 'tis incredible to believe
How much she loves me: O, the kindest Kate!   300
She hung about my neck, and kiss on kiss
She vied so fast, protesting oath on oath,
That in a twink she won me to her love.
O, you are novices! 'Tis a world to see,

How tame, when men and women are alone,
A meacock wretch can make the curstest shrew.
Give me thy hand, Kate. I will unto Venice,
To buy apparel 'gainst the wedding-day.
Provide the feast, father, and bid the guests;
I will be sure my Katherine shall be fine.　　　　310

BAPTISTA I know not what to say; but give me your hands.
God send you joy, Petruchio! 'Tis a match.

GREMIO, TRANIO 'Amen', say we. We will be witnesses.

PETRUCHIO Father, and wife, and gentlemen, adieu.
I will to Venice; Sunday comes apace.
We will have rings, and things, and fine array,
And – kiss me, Kate, 'We will be married o' Sunday'.[77]

　　　　　　　　　[*Exeunt Petruchio and Katherina.*

GREMIO Was ever match clapped up so suddenly?

BAPTISTA Faith, gentlemen, now I play a merchant's part,
And venture madly on a desperate mart.　　　　320

TRANIO 'Twas a commodity lay fretting by you.
'Twill bring you gain, or perish on the seas.

BAPTISTA The gain I seek is quiet in the match.

GREMIO No doubt but he hath got a quiet catch.[78]
But now, Baptista, to your younger daughter:
Now is the day we long have lookèd for.
I am your neighbour, and was suitor first.

TRANIO And I am one that love Bianca more
Than words can witness, or your thoughts can guess.

GREMIO Youngling, thou canst not love so dear as I.　　　　330

TRANIO Greybeard, thy love doth freeze.

GREMIO 　　　　　　　　　　　　　But thine doth fry.
Skipper, stand back; 'tis age that nourisheth.

TRANIO But youth in ladies' eyes that flourisheth.

BAPTISTA Content you, gentlemen; I will compound this strife.
'Tis deeds must win the prize, and he, of both,
That can assure my daughter greatest dower
Shall have my Bianca's love.[79]
Say, Signor Gremio, what can you assure her?

GREMIO First, as you know, my house within the city
Is richly furnishèd with plate and gold,　　　　340
Basins and ewers to lave her dainty hands;

My hangings all of Tyrian tapestry;
In ivory coffers I have stuffed my crowns,
In cypress chests my Arras counterpoints,
Costly apparel, tents and canopies,
Fine linen, Turkey cushions bossed with pearl,
Vallens of Venice gold in needlework,
Pewter and brass, and all things that belongs
To house or housekeeping. Then, at my farm,
I have a hundred milch-kine to the pail,   350
Six-score fat oxen standing in my stalls,
And all things answerable to this portion.
Myself am struck in years, I must confess,
And, if I die tomorrow, this is hers,
If whilst I live she will be only mine.

TRANIO   That 'only' came well in. Sir, list to me:
I am my father's heir and only son.
If I may have your daughter to my wife,
I'll leave her houses three or four as good,
Within rich Pisa walls, as any one   360
Old Signor Gremio has in Padua,
Besides two thousand ducats by the year
Of fruitful land, all which shall be her jointure.
– What, have I pinched you, Signor Gremio?

GREMIO   Two thousand ducats by the year, of land?
[*Aside:*] My land amounts not to so much in all.
[*Aloud:*] That she shall have, besides an argosy
That now is lying in Marcellus' road.
– What, have I choked you with an argosy?

TRANIO   Gremio, 'tis known my father hath no less   370
Than three great argosies, besides two galliasses
And twelve tight galleys. These I will assure her,
And twice as much whate'er thou off'rest next.

GREMIO   Nay, I have offered all; I have no more;
And she can have no more than all I have.
If you like me, she shall have me and mine.

TRANIO   Why, then the maid is mine from all the world,
By your firm promise; Gremio is out-vied.

BAPTISTA I must confess your offer is the best,
And, let your father make her the assurance,   380

            She is your own; else – you must pardon me –
            If you should die before him, where's her dower?

TRANIO   That's but a cavil; he is old, I young.

GREMIO   And may not young men die, as well as old?

BAPTISTA   Well, gentlemen,
            I am thus resolved: on Sunday next, you know,
            My daughter Katherine is to be married;
            [*to Tranio:*] Now, on the Sunday following, shall
                                         Bianca
            Be bride to you, if you make this assurance;
            If not, to Signor Gremio.   390
            – And so I take my leave, and thank you both.
                                            [*Exit.*

GREMIO   Adieu, good neighbour. – Now I fear thee not;
            Sirrah, young gamester, your father were a fool
            To give thee all, and in his waning age
            Set foot under thy table. Tut, a toy!
            An old Italian fox is not so kind, my boy.[80]   [*Exit.*

TRANIO   A vengeance on your crafty withered hide!
            Yet I have faced it with a card of ten.[81]
            'Tis in my head to do my master good:
            I see no reason but supposed Lucentio   400
            Must get a father called (supposed) Vincentio.
            And that's a wonder: fathers commonly
            Do get their children; but, in this case of wooing,
            A child shall get a sire, if I fail not of my cunning.
                                           [*Exit.*

ACT 3, SCENE 1.

Bianca's room in Baptista's house.

Enter LUCENTIO *(with books, as Cambio),* BIANCA *and* HORTENSIO
  (with lute, as Licio). Hortensio tries to lead Bianca aside.

LUCENTIO Fiddler, forbear! You grow too forward, sir![82]
          Have you so soon forgot the entertainment
          Her sister Katherine welcomed you withal?
HORTENSIO But, wrangling pedant, this is[83]
          The patroness of heavenly harmony:
          Then give me leave to have prerogative;
          And when in music we have spent an hour,
          Your lecture shall have leisure for as much.
LUCENTIO Preposterous ass, that never read so far
          To know the cause why music was ordained!   10
          Was it not to refresh the mind of man
          After his studies or his usual pain?
          Then give me leave to read philosophy,
          And while I pause, serve in your harmony.
HORTENSIO Sirrah, I will not bear these braves of thine.
BIANCA   Why, gentlemen, you do me double wrong,
          To strive for that which resteth in my choice.
          I am no breeching scholar in the schools:
          I'll not be tied to hours nor 'pointed times,
          But learn my lessons as I please myself.   20
          And, to cut off all strife, here sit we down:
          Take you your instrument, play you the whiles;
          His lecture will be done ere you have tuned.
HORTENSIO You'll leave his lecture when I am in tune?
LUCENTIO That will be never! Tune your instrument.
                              [*Hortensio tunes it.*

BIANCA   [*to Lucentio:*] Where left we last?
LUCENTIO Here, madam. [*He reads:*]
              '*Hic ibat Simois, hic est Sigeia tellus,*
              Hic steterat Priami regia celsa senis.'[84]
BIANCA   Conster them.   30

LUCENTIO   '*Hic ibat*', as I told you before; '*Simois*', I am Lucentio;
     '*hic est*', son unto Vincentio of Pisa; '*Sigeia tellus*',
     disguised thus to get your love; '*Hic steterat*', and that
     Lucentio that comes a-wooing; '*Priami*', is my man
     Tranio; '*regia*', bearing my port; '*celsa senis*', that we
     might beguile the old pantaloon.[85]

HORTENSIO   Madam, my instrument's in tune.

BIANCA   Let's hear. [*He plays.*] O fie! The treble jars.

LUCENTIO   Spit in the hole, man, and tune again.

                          [*Hortensio tunes again.*

BIANCA   Now let me see if I can conster it. '*Hic ibat Simois*', I   40
     know you not; '*hic est Sigeia tellus*', I trust you not; '*Hic
     steterat Priami*', take heed he hear us not; '*regia*', pre-
     sume not; '*celsa senis*', despair not.

HORTENSIO   Madam, 'tis now in tune.   [*He plays.*

LUCENTIO   All but the bass.

HORTENSIO   The bass is right; 'tis the base knave that jars.
     [*Aside:*] How fiery and forward our pedant is!
     Now, for my life, the knave doth court my love.
     Pedascule, I'll watch you better yet.

BIANCA   In time I may believe, yet I mistrust.

LUCENTIO   Mistrust it not – for, sure, Æacides   50
     Was Ajax, called so from his grandfather.[86]

BIANCA   I must believe my master, else, I promise you,
     I should be arguing still upon that doubt.
     But let it rest. – Now, Licio, to you.
     Good master, take it not unkindly, pray,
     That I have been thus pleasant with you both.[87]

HORTENSIO   [*to Lucentio:*] You may go walk, and give me
                             leave awhile:
     My lessons make no music in three parts.

LUCENTIO   Are you so formal, sir? Well, I must wait –
     [*aside:*] And watch withal, for, but I be deceived,   60
     Our fine musician groweth amorous.

                          [*He moves away.*

HORTENSIO   Madam, before you touch the instrument
     To learn the order of my fingering,
     I must begin with rudiments of art,
     To teach you gamouth[88] in a briefer sort,

        More pleasant, pithy and effectual
        Than hath been taught by any of my trade;
        And there it is in writing, fairly drawn.

BIANCA   Why, I am past my gamouth long ago.

HORTENSIO Yet read the gamouth of Hortensio.   70

BIANCA   [*reads:*] ' "Gamouth" I am, the ground of all accord;
            "*A re*", to plead Hortensio's passion;
             "*B mi*", Bianca, take him for thy lord,
              "*C fa ut*", that loves with all affection;
           "*D sol re*", one clef, two notes have I;
           "*E la mi*", show pity, or I die.'[89]
        Call you this 'gamouth'? Tut! I like it not.
        Old fashions please me best: I am not so nice
        To change true rules for odd inventions.

Enter SERVANT.

SERVANT   Mistress, your father prays you leave your books,   80
        And help to dress your sister's chamber up.
        You know tomorrow is the wedding-day.

BIANCA   Farewell, sweet masters both; I must be gone.
               [*Exeunt Bianca and servant.*

LUCENTIO Faith, mistress, then I have no cause to stay.   [*Exit.*

HORTENSIO But I have cause to pry into this pedant:
        Methinks he looks as though he were in love.
        Yet if thy thoughts, Bianca, be so humble
        To cast thy wand'ring eyes on every stale,
        Seize thee that list! If once I find thee ranging,
        Hortensio will be quit with thee by changing.   90
                    [*Exit.*

SCENE 2.

A street in Padua, outside Baptista's house.

Enter BAPTISTA, GREMIO, TRANIO *(as Lucentio),*
LUCENTIO *(as Cambio),* KATHERINA *(in bridal array),*
BIANCA, GUESTS *and* ATTENDANTS.

BAPTISTA [*to Tranio:*] Signor Lucentio, this is the 'pointed day
That Katherine and Petruchio should be married,
And yet we hear not of our son-in-law.
What will be said? What mockery will it be,
To want the bridegroom when the priest attends
To speak the ceremonial rites of marriage!
What says Lucentio to this shame of ours?

KATHERINA No shame but mine. I must forsooth be forced
To give my hand, opposed against my heart,
Unto a mad-brain rudesby, full of spleen,   10
Who wooed in haste, and means to wed at leisure.[90]
I told you, I, he was a frantic fool,
Hiding his bitter jests in blunt behaviour;
And, to be noted for a merry man,
He'll woo a thousand, 'point the day of marriage,
Make friends, invite them, and proclaim the banes,[91]
Yet never means to wed where he hath wooed.
Now must the world point at poor Katherine,
And say, 'Lo, there is mad Petruchio's wife,
If it would please him come and marry her.'   20

TRANIO Patience, good Katherine, and Baptista too.
Upon my life, Petruchio means but well,
Whatever fortune stays him from his word.
Though he be blunt, I know him passing wise;
Though he be merry, yet withal he's honest.

KATHERINA Would Katharine had never seen him though!
        [*Exeunt Katherina (weeping), Bianca and attendants.*

BAPTISTA Go, girl; I cannot blame thee now to weep,
For such an injury would vex a very saint,
Much more a shrew of impatient humour.[92]

Enter BIONDELLO.

BIONDELLO Master, master! News, and such old news as you never   30
heard of![93]

BAPTISTA Is it new and old too? How may that be?

BIONDELLO Why, is it not news, to hear of Petruchio's coming?

BAPTISTA Is he come?

BIONDELLO Why, no, sir.

BAPTISTA What then?

BIONDELLO He is coming.

BAPTISTA When will he be here?

BIONDELLO When he stands where I am and sees you there.

TRANIO But say, what to thine 'old' news?   40

BIONDELLO Why, Petruchio is coming, in: a new hat and an old
jerkin; a pair of old breeches thrice turned; a pair of
boots that have been candle-cases, one buckled, another
laced; an old rusty sword tane out of the town
armoury, with a broken hilt, and chapeless; with two
broken points; his horse hipped (with an old mothy
saddle and stirrups of no kindred), besides, possessed
with the glanders and like to mose in the chine, troubled
with the lampass, infected with the fashions, full of
windgalls, sped with spavins, rayed with the yellows,   50
past cure of the fives, stark spoiled with the staggers,
begnawn with the bots, swayed in the back and shoulder-
shotten, near-legged before, and with a half-cheeked
bit, and a head-stall of sheep's leather, which, being
restrained to keep him from stumbling, hath been often
burst and now repaired with knots; one girth six times
pieced, and a woman's crupper of velure, which hath
two letters for her name fairly set down in studs, and
here and there pieced with pack-thread.

BAPTISTA Who comes with him?   60

BIONDELLO O sir, his lackey, for all the world caparisoned like the
horse: with a linen stock on one leg, and a kersey boot-
hose on the other, gartered with a red and blue list; an
old hat, and the humour of forty fancies pricked in't for
a feather: a monster, a very monster in apparel, and not
like a Christian footboy or a gentleman's lackey.

TRANIO 'Tis some odd humour pricks him to this fashion;

     Yet oftentimes he goes but mean-apparelled.

BAPTISTA   I am glad he's come, howsoe'er he comes.

BIONDELLO   Why, sir, he comes not.   70

BAPTISTA   Didst thou not say he comes?

BIONDELLO   Who? That Petruchio came?

BAPTISTA   Ay, that Petruchio came.

BIONDELLO   No, sir, I say his horse comes, with him on his back.

BAPTISTA   Why, that's all one.

BIONDELLO   Nay, by Saint Jamy,
           I hold you a penny,
           A horse and a man
           Is more than one,
           And yet not many.[94]   80

Enter PETRUCHIO *and* GRUMIO, *clad as described.*

PETRUCHIO   Come, where be these gallants? Who's at home?

BAPTISTA   You are welcome, sir.

PETRUCHIO   And yet I come not well?

BAPTISTA   And yet you halt not.

TRANIO   Not so well apparelled
     As I wish you were.

PETRUCHIO   Were it not better I should rush in thus?[95]
     But where is Kate? Where is my lovely bride?
     How does my father? Gentles, methinks you frown;
     And wherefore gaze this goodly company
     As if they saw some wondrous monument,
     Some comet or unusual prodigy?   90

BAPTISTA   Why, sir, you know this is your wedding-day.
     First were we sad, fearing you would not come;
     Now sadder, that you come so unprovided.
     Fie! Doff this habit, shame to your estate,
     An eye-sore to our solemn festival.

TRANIO   And tell us what occasion of import
     Hath all so long detained you from your wife,
     And sent you hither so unlike yourself.

PETRUCHIO   Tedious it were to tell, and harsh to hear.
     Sufficeth I am come to keep my word,   100
     Though in some part enforcèd to digress,
     Which at more leisure I will so excuse
     As you shall well be satisfied with all.

But where is Kate? I stay too long from her:
The morning wears, 'tis time we were at church.

TRANIO See not your bride in these unreverent robes.
Go to my chamber, put on clothes of mine.

PETRUCHIO Not I, believe me; thus I'll visit her.

BAPTISTA But thus, I trust, you will not marry her.

PETRUCHIO Good sooth, even thus; therefore ha' done
with words.   110
To me she's married, not unto my clothes.
Could I repair what she will wear in me,
As I can change these poor accoutrements,
'Twere well for Kate and better for myself.[96]
But what a fool am I to chat with you,
When I should bid good morrow to my bride,
And seal the title with a lovely kiss!
                    [*Exit Petruchio and Grumio.*

TRANIO He hath some meaning in his mad attire.
We will persuade him, be it possible,
To put on better ere he go to church.   120

BAPTISTA I'll after him, and see the event of this.
          [*Exeunt Baptista, Gremio, Biondello and attendants.*

TRANIO [*to Lucentio:*] But, sir, to love concerneth us to add[97]
Her father's liking, which to bring to pass,
As I before imparted to your Worship,
I am to get a man (whate'er he be,
It skills not much; we'll fit him to our turn),
And he shall be Vincentio of Pisa,
And make assurance here in Padua
Of greater sums than I have promisèd.
So shall you quietly enjoy your hope,   130
And marry sweet Bianca with consent.

LUCENTIO Were it not that my fellow-schoolmaster
Doth watch Bianca's steps so narrowly,
'Twere good methinks to steal our marriage,[98]
Which once performed, let all the world say 'no',
I'll keep mine own despite of all the world.

TRANIO That by degrees we mean to look into,
And watch our vantage in this business.
We'll over-reach the greybeard, Gremio,

The narrow-prying father, Minola,   140
The quaint musician, amorous Licio,
All for my master's sake, Lucentio.

Enter GREMIO.

Signor Gremio, came you from the church?
GREMIO   As willingly as e'er I came from school.
TRANIO   And is the bride and bridegroom coming home?
GREMIO   A 'bridegroom', say you? 'Tis a groom, indeed,
A grumbling groom, and that the girl shall find.
TRANIO   Curster than she? Why, 'tis impossible.
GREMIO   Why, he's a devil, a devil, a very fiend.
TRANIO   Why, she's a devil, a devil, the devil's dam.   150
GREMIO   Tut! She's a lamb, a dove, a fool, to him.
I'll tell you, Sir Lucentio: when the priest
Should ask if Katherine should be his wife,
'Ay, by Gog's wouns!', quoth he, and swore so loud
That, all-amazed, the priest let fall the book,
And, as be stooped again to take it up,
This mad-brained bridegroom took him such a cuff
That down fell priest and book, and book and priest.
'Now take them up', quoth he, 'if any list.'
TRANIO   What said the wench, when he rose again?[99]   160
GREMIO   Trembled and shook; for why, he stamped and swore,
As if the vicar meant to cozen him.
But after many ceremonies done,
He calls for wine: 'A health!', quoth he, as if
He had been aboard, carousing to his mates
After a storm; quaffed off the muscadel,
And threw the sops all in the sexton's face,
Having no other reason
But that his beard grew thin and hungerly,
And seemed to ask him sops as he was drinking.   170
This done, he took the bride about the neck,
And kissed her lips with such a clamorous smack
That at the parting all the church did echo;
And I, seeing this, came thence for very shame,
And after me, I know, the rout is coming.
Such a mad marriage never was before!   [*Music heard*.
Hark, hark! I hear the minstrels play.[100]

Enter PETRUCHIO *and* KATHERINA, *followed by* BIANCA, BAPTISTA,
HORTENSIO *(as Licio),* GRUMIO, MINSTRELS *and* OTHERS.
Music concludes.

PETRUCHIO Gentlemen and friends, I thank you for your pains.
I know you think to dine with me today,
And have prepared great store of wedding cheer;   180
But so it is, my haste doth call me hence,
And therefore here I mean to take my leave.

BAPTISTA Is't possible you will away tonight?

PETRUCHIO I must away today before night come.
Make it no wonder; if you knew my business,
You would entreat me rather go than stay;
And, honest company, I thank you all,
That have beheld me give away myself
To this most patient, sweet and virtuous wife.
Dine with my father, drink a health to me,   190
For I must hence, and farewell to you all.

TRANIO Let us entreat you stay till after dinner.

PETRUCHIO It may not be.

GREMIO   Let me entreat you.

PETRUCHIO It cannot be.

KATHERINA   Let me entreat you.

PETRUCHIO I am content.

KATHERINA   Are you content to stay?

PETRUCHIO I am content you shall entreat me stay –
But yet not stay, entreat me how you can.

KATHERINA Now, if you love me, stay.

PETRUCHIO   Grumio, my horse.

GRUMIO Ay, sir, they be ready: the oats have eaten the horses.[101]

KATHERINA Nay then,   200
Do what thou canst, I will not go today,
No, nor tomorrow, not till I please myself.
The door is open, sir; there lies your way:
You may be jogging whiles your boots are green.[102]
For me, I'll not be gone till I please myself.
'Tis like you'll prove a jolly surly groom,
That take it on you at the first so roundly.

PETRUCHIO O, Kate, content thee; prithee, be not angry.

KATHERINA I will be angry; what hast thou to do?

                   – Father, be quiet; he shall stay my leisure.[103]   210
GREMIO   Ay, marry, sir; now it begins to work.
KATHERINA Gentlemen, forward to the bridal dinner.
                   I see a woman may be made a fool,
                   If she had not a spirit to resist.
PETRUCHIO They shall go forward, Kate, at thy command.
                   – Obey the bride, you that attend on her!
                   Go to the feast, revel and domineer,
                   Carouse full measure to her maidenhead,
                   Be mad and merry, or go hang yourselves;
                   But, for my bonny Kate, she must with me.   220
                   Nay, look not big, nor stamp, nor stare, nor fret;
                   I will be master of what is mine own.
                   She is my goods, my chattels; she is my house,
                   My household stuff, my field, my barn,
                   My horse, my ox, my ass, my anything;[104]
                   And here she stands: touch her whoever dare!
                   I'll bring mine action on the proudest he
                   That stops my way in Padua. – Grumio,
                   Draw forth thy weapon, we are beset with thieves.
                   Rescue thy mistress, if thou be a man. –   230
                   Fear not, sweet wench, they shall not touch thee, Kate;
                   I'll buckler thee against a million!
                               [*Exeunt Petruchio, Katherina and Grumio.*
BAPTISTA   Nay, let them go – a couple of quiet ones!
GREMIO   Went they not quickly, I should die with laughing.
TRANIO   Of all mad matches, never was the like!
LUCENTIO   Mistress, what's your opinion of your sister?
BIANCA   That, being mad herself, she's madly mated.
GREMIO   I warrant him, Petruchio is Kated.
BAPTISTA   Neighbours and friends, though bride and
                                              bridegroom wants
                   For to supply the places at the table,   240
                   You know there wants no junkets at the feast.
                   – Lucentio, you shall supply the bridegroom's place,
                   And let Bianca take her sister's room.
TRANIO   Shall sweet Bianca practise how to bride it?
BAPTISTA   She shall, Lucentio. Come, gentlemen, let's go.
                               [*Exeunt.*

ACT 4, SCENE I.

The hall of Petruchio's house in the countryside.

Enter GRUMIO.

GRUMIO   Fie, fie, on all tired jades, on all mad masters, and all foul ways! Was ever man so beaten? Was ever man so rayed? Was ever man so weary? I am sent before to make a fire, and they are coming after to warm them. Now, were not I a little pot and soon hot,[105] my very lips might freeze to my teeth, my tongue to the roof of my mouth, my heart in my belly, ere I should come by a fire to thaw me. But I, with blowing the fire, shall warm myself; for, considering the weather, a taller man than I will take cold. Holla, ho! Curtis!   10

Enter CURTIS.

CURTIS   Who is that calls so coldly?

GRUMIO   A piece of ice. If thou doubt it, thou mayst slide from my shoulder to my heel with no greater a run but my head and my neck. A fire, good Curtis.

CURTIS   Is my master and his wife coming, Grumio?

GRUMIO   O ay, Curtis, ay – and therefore fire, fire! Cast on no water.[106]

CURTIS   Is she so hot a shrew as she's reported?

GRUMIO   She was, good Curtis, before this frost; but thou know'st winter tames man, woman, and beast:[107] for it   20 hath tamed my old master, and my new mistress, and myself, fellow Curtis.

CURTIS   Away, you three-inch fool! I am no beast.

GRUMIO   Am I but three inches? Why, thy horn is a foot, and so long am I at the least.[108] But wilt thou make a fire, or shall I complain on thee to our mistress, whose hand (she being now at hand) thou shalt soon feel, to thy cold comfort, for being slow in thy hot office?

CURTIS   [*while kindling a fire:*] I prithee, good Grumio, tell me, how goes the world?   30

GRUMIO   A cold world, Curtis, in every office but thine – and therefore fire. Do thy duty, and have thy duty, for my master and mistress are almost frozen to death.

CURTIS   [*rising from the hearth:*] There's fire ready; and therefore, good Grumio, the news?

GRUMIO   Why, 'Jack boy, ho boy!', and as much news as wilt thou.[109]

CURTIS   Come, you are so full of cony-catching.

GRUMIO   Why, therefore fire, for I have caught extreme cold. Where's the cook? Is supper ready, the house trimmed,   40 rushes strewed, cobwebs swept, the serving-men in their new fustian, the white stockings, and every officer his wedding-garment on? Be the Jacks fair within, the Jills fair without,[110] the carpets laid, and everything in order?

CURTIS   All ready; and therefore, I pray thee, news.

GRUMIO   First, know, my horse is tired, my master and mistress fallen out –

CURTIS   How?

GRUMIO   Out of their saddles into the dirt, and thereby hangs a   50 tale.

CURTIS   Let's ha't, good Grumio.

GRUMIO   Lend thine ear.

CURTIS   Here.

GRUMIO   [*striking Curtis's ear:*] There!

CURTIS   This 'tis to feel a tale, not to hear a tale.

GRUMIO   And therefore 'tis called a sensible tale;[111] and this cuff was but to knock at your ear and beseech listening. Now I begin. *Imprimis*, we came down a foul hill, my master riding behind my mistress –   60

CURTIS   Both of one horse?

GRUMIO   What's that to thee?

CURTIS   Why, a horse.

GRUMIO   Tell *thou* the tale! But hadst thou not crossed me, thou shouldst have heard how her horse fell, and she under her horse; thou shouldst have heard in how miry a place, how she was bemoiled, how he left her with the horse upon her, how he beat me because her horse stumbled, how she waded through the dirt to pluck him off me; how he swore, how she prayed that never   70 prayed before; how I cried, how the horses ran away,

how her bridle was burst, how I lost my crupper – with
many things of worthy memory, which now shall die in
oblivion, and thou return unexperienced to thy grave.

CURTIS   By this reck'ning, he is more shrew than she.

GRUMIO   Ay, and that thou and the proudest of you all shall find
when he comes home. But what talk I of this? Call forth
Nathaniel, Joseph, Nicholas, Philip, Walter, Sugarsop
and the rest; let their heads be slickly combed, their blue
coats brushed, and their garters of an indifferent knit; let   80
them curtsy with their left legs, and not presume to
touch a hair of my master's horse-tail till they kiss their
hands.[112] Are they all ready?

CURTIS   They are.

GRUMIO   Call them forth.

CURTIS   [calls:] Do you hear, ho? You must meet my master to
countenance my mistress.

GRUMIO   Why, she hath a face of her own.

CURTIS   Who knows not that?

GRUMIO   Thou, it seems, that calls for company to countenance   90
her.

CURTIS   I call them forth to credit her.

GRUMIO   Why, she comes to borrow nothing of them.[113]

Enter NATHANIEL, PHILIP, JOSEPH, NICHOLAS *and* GREGORY. [114]

NATH.   Welcome home, Grumio.

PHILIP   How now, Grumio?

JOSEPH   What, Grumio!

NICHOLAS   Fellow Grumio!

NATH.   How now, old lad?

GRUMIO   Welcome, you! – How now, you? – What, you! –
Fellow, you! – And thus much for greeting. Now, my   100
spruce companions, is all ready, and all things neat?

NATH.   All things is ready. How near is our master?

GRUMIO   E'en at hand, alighted by this; and therefore be not –
Cock's passion, silence! I hear my master.

Enter PETRUCHIO *and* KATHERINA, *both muddy.*

PETRUCHIO Where be these knaves? What, no man at door[115]
To hold my stirrup, nor to take my horse?
Where is Nathaniel, Gregory, Philip?

SERVANTS   [*all responding:*] Here! – Here sir! – Here sir!

PETRUCHIO   'Here sir! Here sir! Here sir! Here sir!' –

     You logger-headed and unpolished grooms!   110

     What, no attendance? No regard? No duty?

     Where is the foolish knave I sent before?

GRUMIO   Here, sir, as foolish as I was before.

PETRUCHIO You peasant swain! You whoreson malt-horse

                                  drudge![116]

     Did I not bid thee meet me in the park,

     And bring along these rascal knaves with thee?

GRUMIO   Nathaniel's coat, sir, was not fully made,

     And Gabr'el's pumps were all unpinked i'th'heel;

     There was no link to colour Peter's hat,

     And Walter's dagger was not come from sheathing.   120

     There were none fine but Adam, Rafe and Gregory;

     The rest were ragged, old and beggarly.

     Yet, as they are, here are they come to meet you.

PETRUCHIO Go, rascals, go, and fetch my supper in.

                                     [*Exeunt servants.*

     [*He sings:*]   'Where is the life that late I led?

                 Where are those' – [117]

     Sit down, Kate, and welcome. Food, food, food, food! [118]

          Enter SERVANTS *with supper.*

     Why, when, I say? – Nay, good sweet Kate, be merry.

     – Off with my boots, you rogues! You villains, when?

                [*A servant kneels to take off his boots.*

     [*He sings:*]   'It was the friar of orders grey,   130

                 As he forth walkèd on his way' –

     Out, you rogue! You pluck my foot awry!

                       [*He kicks the servant.*[119]

     Take that, and mend the plucking of the other.

                    [*The second boot is removed.*

     – Be merry, Kate. – Some water here! What ho!

          Enter SERVANT *with water.*

     Where's my spaniel Troilus? Sirrah, get you hence,

     And bid my cousin Ferdinand come hither –

                          [*Exit servant.*

     One, Kate, that you must kiss, and be acquainted with.

     – Where are my slippers? Shall I have some water?

                     [*A basin is offered to him.*

     – Come, Kate, and wash, and welcome heartily.

                  [*He makes the servant spill the water.*

     – You whoreson villain! Will you let it fall?   140

                       [*He strikes the servant.*

KATHERINA Patience, I pray you: 'twas a fault unwilling.

PETRUCHIO A whoreson, beetle-headed, flap-eared knave!

     Come, Kate, sit down; I know you have a stomach.

                      [*She sits at the table.*

     Will you give thanks, sweet Kate, or else shall I? –

     What's this? Mutton?

SERVANT I   Ay.

PETRUCHIO   Who brought it?

PETER   I.

PETRUCHIO 'Tis burnt, and so is all the meat.

     What dogs are these! Where is the rascal cook?

     How durst you villains bring it from the dresser

     And serve it thus to me that love it not?

     There, take it to you, trenchers, cups and all!   150

              [*He throws the meal at the servants.*

     You heedless joltheads and unmannered slaves!

     What, do you grumble? I'll be with you straight.

                   [*Exeunt servants.*

KATHERINA I pray you, husband, be not so disquiet;

     The meat was well, if you were so contented.

PETRUCHIO I tell thee, Kate, 'twas burnt and dried away,

     And I expressly am forbid to touch it:

     For it engenders choler, planteth anger,

     And better 'twere that both of us did fast –

     Since, of ourselves, ourselves are choleric –

     Than feed it with such over-roasted flesh.   160

     Be patient; tomorrow't shall be mended,

     And, for this night, we'll fast for company.

     Come, I will bring thee to thy bridal chamber.

                       [*Exeunt.*

    Enter (separately) SERVANTS, *including* NATHANIEL,

           PETER *and* GRUMIO.

NATH.   Peter, didst ever see the like?

PETER   He kills her in her own humour.

Enter CURTIS.

GRUMIO   Where is he?

CURTIS   In her chamber,
          Making a sermon of continency to her,
          And rails and swears and rates, that she (poor soul)
          Knows not which way to stand, to look, to speak,   170
          And sits as one new-risen from a dream.
          Away, away, for he is coming hither![120]

                                                        [*Exeunt.*

Enter PETRUCHIO.

PETRUCHIO Thus have I póliticly begun my reign,
          And 'tis my hope to end successfully.
          My falcon now is sharp and passing empty,
          And, till she stoop, she must not be full-gorged,
          For then she never looks upon her lure.
          Another way I have to man my haggard,
          To make her come and know her keeper's call:
          That is, to watch her, as we watch these kites   180
          That bate and beat and will not be obedient.
          She ate no meat today, nor none shall eat;
          Last night she slept not,[121] nor tonight she shall not;
          As with the meat, some undeservèd fault
          I'll find about the making of the bed,
          And here I'll fling the pillow, there the bolster,
          This way the coverlet, another way the sheets:
          Ay, and amid this hurly I intend
          That all is done in reverend care of her.
          And, in conclusion, she shall watch all night,   190
          And, if she chance to nod, I'll rail and brawl,
          And with the clamour keep her still awake.
          This is a way to kill a wife with kindness;
          And thus I'll curb her mad and headstrong humour.
          He that knows better how to tame a shrew,
          Now let him speak:[122] 'tis charity to show.

                                                        [*Exit.*

SCENE 2.

A street in Padua, outside Baptista's house.

Enter TRANIO *(as Lucentio) and* HORTENSIO *(as Licio).*

TRANIO   Is't possible, friend Licio, that Mistress Bianca
            Doth fancy any other but Lucentio?
            I tell you, sir, she bears me fair in hand.
HORTENSIO Sir, to satisfy you in what I have said,
            Stand by, and mark the manner of his teaching.
                                        [*They stand aside.*

Enter LUCENTIO *(as Cambio) and* BIANCA.

LUCENTIO Now, mistress, profit you in what you read?
BIANCA   What, master, read *you*? First resolve me that.
LUCENTIO I read that I profess, *The Art to Love*.[123]
BIANCA   And may you prove, sir, master of your art.
LUCENTIO While you, sweet dear, prove mistress of my heart.   10
                                        [*They kiss and court.*
HORTENSIO Quick proceeders, marry! Now, tell me, I pray,
            You that durst swear that your mistress Bianca
            Loved none in the world so well as Lucentio.
TRANIO   O despiteful love! Unconstant womankind!
            I tell thee, Licio, this is wonderful.
HORTENSIO Mistake no more: I am not Licio,
            Nor a musician, as I seem to be,
            But one that scorn to live in this disguise
            For such a one as leaves a gentleman
            And makes a god of such a cullion.   20
            Know, sir, that I am called Hortensio.
TRANIO   Signor Hortensio, I have often heard
            Of your entire affection to Bianca,[124]
            And since mine eyes are witness of her lightness,
            I will with you, if you be so contented,
            Forswear Bianca and her love for ever.
HORTENSIO See, how they kiss and court! Signor Lucentio,
            Here is my hand, and here I firmly vow
            Never to woo her more, but do forswear her
            As one unworthy all the former favours   30

That I have fondly flattered her withal.

TRANIO And here I take the like unfeignèd oath,
Never to marry with her, though she would entreat.
Fie on her! See, how beastly she doth court him.

HORTENSIO Would all the world but he had quite forsworn!125
For me, that I may surely keep mine oath,
I will be married to a wealthy widow,
Ere three days pass, which hath as long loved me
As I have loved this proud disdainful haggard.
And so farewell, Signor Lucentio. 40
Kindness in women, not their beauteous looks,
Shall win my love; and so I take my leave,
In resolution as I swore before.

[*Exit. Tranio joins Bianca and Lucentio.*

TRANIO Mistress Bianca, bless you with such grace
As 'longeth to a lover's blessèd case!
Nay, I have tane you napping, gentle love,
And have forsworn you, with Hortensio.

BIANCA Tranio, you jest — but have you both forsworn me?

TRANIO Mistress, we have.

LUCENTIO   Then we are rid of Licio.

TRANIO I'faith, he'll have a lusty widow now, 50
That shall be wooed and wedded in a day.

BIANCA God give him joy!

TRANIO Ay, and he'll tame her.

BIANCA   He says so, Tranio?

TRANIO Faith, he is gone unto the taming school.

BIANCA 'The taming school'! What, is there such a place?

TRANIO Ay, mistress, and Petruchio is the master,
That teacheth tricks eleven-and-twenty long,126
To tame a shrew and charm her chattering tongue.

Enter BIONDELLO.

BIONDELLO O master, master, I have watched so long
That I am dog-weary, but at last I spied 60
An ancient angel, coming down the hill,
Will serve the turn.

TRANIO   What is he, Biondello?

BIONDELLO Master, a marcantant, or a pedant,127

I know not what; but formal in apparel,
In gait and countenance surely like a father.

LUCENTIO And what of him, Tranio?

TRANIO If he be credulous and trust my tale,
I'll make him glad to seem Vincentio,
And give assurance to Baptista Minola
As if he were the right Vincentio.   70
Take in your love, and then let me alone.[128]

> [*Lucentio and Bianca enter Baptista's house.*

> *Enter* PEDANT.

PEDANT God save you, sir.

TRANIO   And you, sir. You are welcome.
Travel you far on, or are you at the farthest?

PEDANT Sir, at the farthest for a week or two,
But then up farther, and as far as Rome,
And so to Tripoli, if God lend me life.

TRANIO What countryman, I pray?

PEDANT   Of Mantua.

TRANIO Of Mantua, sir? Marry, God forbid!
And come to Padua, careless of your life?

PEDANT My life, sir? How, I pray? For that goes hard.   80

TRANIO 'Tis death for anyone in Mantua
To come to Padua. Know you not the cause?
Your ships are stayed at Venice, and the Duke –
For private quarrel 'twixt your Duke and him –
Hath published and proclaimed it openly.
'Tis marvel; but that you are but newly come,
You might have heard it else proclaimed about.

PEDANT Alas, sir, it is worse for me than so,
For I have bills for money by exchange
From Florence, and must here deliver them.   90

TRANIO Well, sir, to do you courtesy,
This will I do, and this I will advise you –
First tell me, have you ever been at Pisa?

PEDANT Ay, sir, in Pisa have I often been,
Pisa renownèd for grave citizens.

TRANIO Among them, know you one Vincentio?

PEDANT I know him not, but I have heard of him:

A merchant of incomparable wealth.

TRANIO He is my father, sir, and sooth to say,
In count'nance somewhat doth resemble you. 100

BIONDELLO [*aside:*] As much as an apple doth an oyster, and all one.

TRANIO To save your life in this extremity,
This favour will I do you for his sake
(And think it not the worst of all your fortunes
That you are like to Sir Vincentio):
His name and credit shall you undertake,
And in my house you shall be friendly lodged.
Look that you take upon you as you should –
You understand me, sir? So shall you stay
Till you have done your business in the city: 110
If this be court'sy, sir, accept of it.

PEDANT O sir, I do, and will repute you ever
The patron of my life and liberty.

TRANIO Then go with me to make the matter good.
This, by the way, I let you understand:
My father is here looked for every day,
To pass assurance of a dower in marriage
'Twixt me and one Baptista's daughter here.
In all these circumstances I'll instruct you.
Go with me to clothe you as becomes you.[129] 120

[*Exeunt.*

SCENE 3.

The hall of Petruchio's house in the countryside.

Enter KATHERINA *and* GRUMIO.

GRUMIO   No, no, forsooth, I dare not for my life.

KATHERINA The more my wrong, the more his spite appears.[130]
          What, did he marry me to famish me?
          Beggars that come unto my father's door
          Upon entreaty have a present alms;
          If not, elsewhere they meet with charity;
          But I, who never knew how to entreat,
          Nor never needed that I should entreat,
          Am starved for meat, giddy for lack of sleep,
          With oaths kept waking, and with brawling fed;   10
          And that which spites me more than all these wants,
          He does it under name of perfect love,
          As who should say, if I should sleep or eat,
          'Twere deadly sickness or else present death.
          I prithee go and get me some repast:
          I care not what, so it be wholesome food.

GRUMIO   What say you to a neat's foot?

KATHERINA 'Tis passing good; I prithee let me have it.

GRUMIO   I fear it is too choleric a meat.
          How say you to a fat tripe finely broiled?   20

KATHERINA I like it well; good Grumio, fetch it me.

GRUMIO   I cannot tell; I fear 'tis choleric.
          What say you to a piece of beef and mustard?

KATHERINA A dish that I do love to feed upon.

GRUMIO   Ay, but the mustard is too hot a little.

KATHERINA Why then, the beef, and let the mustard rest.

GRUMIO   Nay then, I will not. You shall have the mustard,
          Or else you get no beef of Grumio.

KATHERINA Then both or one, or anything thou wilt.

GRUMIO   Why then, the mustard without the beef.   30

KATHERINA Go, get thee gone, thou false deluding slave,

                                  [*She beats him.*
          That feed'st me with the very name of meat!

       Sorrow on thee and all the pack of you
       That triumph thus upon my misery!
       Go, get thee gone, I say.

Enter PETRUCHIO *(bearing food on a dish) and* HORTENSIO.

PETRUCHIO How fares my Kate? What, sweeting, all amort?
HORTENSIO Mistress, what cheer?
KATHERINA   Faith, as cold as can be.
PETRUCHIO Pluck up thy spirits; look cheerfully upon me.
       Here, love, thou seest how diligent I am,
       To dress thy meat myself and bring it thee.   40
              [*He sets the dish down. She eats hungrily.*[131]
       I am sure, sweet Kate, this kindness merits thanks.
       What, not a word? Nay then, thou lov'st it not,
       And all my pains is sorted to no proof.[132]
                    [*He snatches the dish.*
       – Here, take away this dish.
KATHERINA   I pray you, let it stand.
PETRUCHIO The poorest service is repaid with thanks,
       And so shall mine before you touch the meat.
KATHERINA I thank you, sir.   [*He replaces the dish.*
HORTENSIO Signor Petruchio, fie! You are to blame.
       Come, Mistress Kate, I'll bear you company.
                    [*He eats from her dish.*
PETRUCHIO [*aside:*] Eat it up all, Hortensio, if thou lov'st me: 50
       Much good do it unto thy gentle heart.
       [*Aloud:*] Kate, eat apace; and now, my honey love,
       Will we return unto thy father's house,
       And revel it as bravely as the best,
       With silken coats and caps, and golden rings,
       With ruffs and cuffs and fardingales, and things;
       With scarfs and fans, and double change of brav'ry,
       With amber bracelets, beads, and all this knav'ry.
       What, hast thou dined? The tailor stays thy leisure,
       To deck thy body with his ruffling treasure.   60

          Enter TAILOR, *bearing a gown.*

       Come, tailor, let us see these ornaments.
       Lay forth the gown.
               [*The tailor displays the gown.*

Enter HABERDASHER, *holding a cap.*

PETRUCHIO   What news with you, sir?

HABER.   Here is the cap your Worship did bespeak.

PETRUCHIO Why, this was moulded on a porringer –
A velvet dish! Fie, fie! 'Tis lewd and filthy;
Why, 'tis a cockle or a walnut-shell,
A knack, a toy, a trick, a baby's cap:
Away with it! Come, let me have a bigger.

KATHERINA I'll have no bigger; this doth fit the time,
And gentlewomen wear such caps as these.   70

PETRUCHIO When you are gentle, you shall have one too,
And not till then.

HORTENSIO [*aside:*]   That will not be in haste.

KATHERINA Why, sir, I trust I may have leave to speak,
And speak I will! I am no child, no babe;
Your betters have endured me say my mind,
And if you cannot, best you stop your ears.
My tongue will tell the anger of my heart,
Or else my heart, concealing it, will break;
And rather than it shall, I will be free,
Even to the uttermost, as I please, in words.   80

PETRUCHIO Why, thou say'st true: it is a paltry cap,
A custard-coffin, a bauble, a silken pie!
I love thee well, in that thou lik'st it not.

KATHERINA Love me or love me not, I like the cap,
And it I will have, or I will have none.

PETRUCHIO Thy gown? Why, ay: come, tailor, let us see't.

                            [*Exit haberdasher.*

O mercy, God! What masquing-stuff is here?
What's this? A sleeve? 'Tis like a demi-cannon.
What? Up and down carved like an apple-tart?
Here's snip and nip and cut and slish and slash,   90
Like to a censer in a barber's shop;[133]
Why, what a devil's name, tailor, call'st thou this?

HORTENSIO [*aside:*] I see she's like to have neither cap nor gown.

TAILOR   You bid me make it orderly and well,
According to the fashion and the time.

PETRUCHIO Marry, and did; but if you be remembered,
I did not bid you mar it to the time.

Go, hop me over every kennel home,
For you shall hop without my custom, sir:
I'll none of it; hence, make your best of it.   100

KATHERINA I never saw a better-fashioned gown,
More quaint, more pleasing, nor more cómmendable.
Belike you mean to make a puppet of me.

PETRUCHIO Why, true, he means to make a puppet of thee.

TAILOR She says your Worship means to make a puppet of her.

PETRUCHIO O monstrous arrogance! Thou liest, thou thread,
                                                        thou thimble,
Thou yard, three-quarters, half-yard, quarter, nail,
Thou flea, thou nit, thou winter-cricket thou!
Braved in mine own house with a skein of thread?
Away, thou rag, thou quantity, thou remnant,   110
Or I shall so be-mete thee with thy yard
As thou shalt think on prating whilst thou liv'st![134]
I tell thee, I, that thou hast marred her gown.

TAILOR Your Worship is deceived; the gown is made
Just as my master had direction:
Grumio gave order how it should be done.

GRUMIO I gave him no order; I gave him the stuff.

TAILOR But how did you desire it should be made?

GRUMIO Marry, sir, with needle and thread.

TAILOR But did you not request to have it cut?   120

GRUMIO Thou hast faced many things.

TAILOR I have.

GRUMIO Face not me. Thou hast braved many men; brave not
me. I will neither be faced nor braved.[135] I say unto
thee, I bid thy master cut out the gown, but I did not
bid him cut it to pieces. *Ergo*, thou liest.

TAILOR Why, here is the note of the fashion to testify.

PETRUCHIO Read it.

GRUMIO The note lies in's throat, if he say I said so.

TAILOR [*reads:*] '*Imprimis*, a loose-bodied gown.'   130

GRUMIO Master, if ever I said 'loose-bodied gown', sew me in
the skirts of it, and beat me to death with a bottom of
brown thread: I said 'a gown'.[136]

PETRUCHIO Proceed.

TAILOR 'With a small compassed cape.'

GRUMIO   I confess the cape.

TAILOR   'With a trunk sleeve.'

GRUMIO   I confess two sleeves.

TAILOR   'The sleeves curiously cut.'

PETRUCHIO   Ay, there's the villainy.   140

GRUMIO   [to tailor:] Error i'th'bill, sir, error i'th'bill! I commanded
            the sleeves should be cut out and sewed up again, and
            that I'll prove upon thee, though thy little finger be
            armed in a thimble.

TAILOR   This is true that I say. And I had thee in place where,
            thou shouldst know it.

GRUMIO   I am for thee straight: take thou the bill, give me thy
            mete-yard, and spare not me.[137]

HORTENSIO   God-a-mercy, Grumio! Then he shall have no odds.

PETRUCHIO   Well, sir, in brief, the gown is not for me.   150

GRUMIO   You are i'th'right, sir: 'tis for my mistress.

PETRUCHIO   [to tailor:] Go, take it up unto thy master's use.

GRUMIO   [to tailor:] Villain, not for thy life! Take up my mistress'
            gown for thy master's use![138]

PETRUCHIO   [to Grumio:] Why, sir, what's your conceit in that?

GRUMIO   O, sir, the conceit is deeper than you think for.
            Take up my mistress' gown to his master's use!
            O, fie, fie, fie!

PETRUCHIO   [aside:] Hortensio, say thou wilt see the tailor paid.
            [To tailor:] Go take it hence, be gone, and say no more.   160

HORTENSIO   [aside:] Tailor, I'll pay thee for thy gown tomorrow.
            Take no unkindness of his hasty words.
            Away, I say. Commend me to thy master.

                                                       [Exit tailor.

PETRUCHIO   Well, come, my Kate; we will unto your father's
            Even in these honest mean habiliments:
            Our purses shall be proud, our garments poor,
            For 'tis the mind that makes the body rich;
            And as the sun breaks through the darkest clouds,
            So honour peereth in the meanest habit.
            What, is the jay more precious than the lark,   170
            Because his feathers are more beautiful?
            Or is the adder better than the eel,
            Because his painted skin contents the eye?

    O no, good Kate; neither art thou the worse
    For this poor furniture and mean array.
    If thou account'st it shame, lay it on me;
    And therefore, frolic, we will hence forthwith,[139]
    To feast and sport us at thy father's house.
    [*To Grumio:*] Go, call my men, and let us straight to
                                     him,
    And bring our horses unto Long Lane end.   180
    There will we mount, and thither walk on foot.
    Let's see, I think 'tis now some seven o'clock,
    And well we may come there by dinner-time.
KATHERINA I dare assure you, sir, 'tis almost two,
    And 'twill be supper-time ere you come there.[140]
PETRUCHIO It shall be seven ere I go to horse.
    Look, what I speak, or do, or think to do,
    You are still crossing it. – Sirs, let't alone:
    I will not go today; and, ere I do,
    It shall be what o'clock I say it is.   190
HORTENSIO [*aside:*] Why, so this gallant will command the sun.
                                    [*Exeunt.*

SCENE 4.

A street in Padua, outside Baptista's house.

Enter TRANIO *(as Lucentio) with the* PEDANT *(booted and bare-headed, dressed as Vincentio).*[141]

TRANIO Sir, this is the house. Please it you that I call?

PEDANT Ay, what else? And but I be deceived,
Signor Baptista may remember me,
Near twenty years ago, in Genoa,
Where we were lodgers at the Pegasus.[142]

TRANIO 'Tis well; and hold your own, in any case,
With such austerity as 'longeth to a father.

PEDANT I warrant you.

Enter BIONDELLO.

But, sir, here comes your boy;
'Twere good he were schooled.

TRANIO Fear you not him. – Sirrah Biondello,   10
Now do your duty throughly, I advise you:
Imagine 'twere the right Vincentio.

BIONDELLO Tut, fear not me.

TRANIO But hast thou done thy errand to Baptista?

BIONDELLO I told him that your father was at Venice,
And that you looked for him this day in Padua.

TRANIO Th'art a tall fellow; hold thee that to drink.

[He gives him money.

Enter BAPTISTA, *followed by* LUCENTIO *(as Cambio).*

[*To pedant:*] Here comes Baptista. Set your
                                                    countenance, sir.
– Signor Baptista, you are happily met.
[*To pedant:*] Sir, this is the gentleman I told you of.   20
I pray you, stand good father to me now:
Give me Bianca for my patrimony.

PEDANT Soft, son.
[*To Baptista:*] Sir, by your leave, having come to Padua
To gather in some debts, my son Lucentio
Made me acquainted with a weighty cause

Of love between your daughter and himself;
And – for the good report I hear of you,
And for the love he beareth to your daughter,
And she to him, – to stay him not too long,   30
I am content, in a good father's care,
To have him matched; and, if you please to like
No worse than I, upon some agreement
Me shall you find ready and willing
With one consent to have her so bestowed:
For curious I cannot be with you,
Signor Baptista, of whom I hear so well.

BAPTISTA Sir, pardon me in what I have to say
(Your plainness and your shortness please me well):
Right true it is, your son Lucentio here   40
Doth love my daughter, and she loveth him,
Or both dissemble deeply their affections;
And therefore, if you say no more than this,
That like a father you will deal with him,
And pass my daughter a sufficient dower,
The match is made, and all is done:
Your son shall have my daughter with consent.

TRANIO I thank you, sir. Where then do you know best
We be affied and such assurance tane
As shall with either part's agreement stand?   50

BAPTISTA Not in my house, Lucentio, for you know
Pitchers have ears, and I have many servants;[143]
Besides, old Gremio is heark'ning still,
And happily we might be interrupted.

TRANIO Then at my lodging, and it like you.
There doth my father lie; and there this night
We'll pass the business privately and well.
Send for your daughter by your servant here.
          [*He indicates Lucentio and winks at him.*[144]
My boy shall fetch the scrivener presently.
The worst is this, that at so slender warning,   60
You are like to have a thin and slender pittance.

BAPTISTA It likes me well. Cambio, hie you home,
And bid Bianca make her ready straight,
And, if you will, tell what hath happenèd:

Lucentio's father is arrived in Padua,
And how she's like to be Lucentio's wife.

[*Exit Lucentio.*

BIONDELLO I pray the gods she may, with all my heart!
TRANIO Dally not with the gods, but get thee gone.

[*Exit Biondello.*

Enter PETER, *a servant.*[145]

Signor Baptista, shall I lead the way?
Welcome. One mess is like to be your cheer.   70
Come sir, we will better it in Pisa.
BAPTISTA I follow you.

[*Exeunt.*

Enter LUCENTIO *(as Cambio) and* BIONDELLO.

BIONDELLO Cambio.
LUCENTIO   What say'st thou, Biondello?
BIONDELLO You saw my master wink and laugh upon you?
LUCENTIO Biondello, what of that?
BIONDELLO Faith, nothing; but has left me here behind, to ex-
          pound the meaning or moral of his signs and tokens.
LUCENTIO I pray thee, moralise them.
BIONDELLO Then thus: Baptista is safe, talking with the deceiving
          father of a deceitful son.   80
LUCENTIO And what of him?
BIONDELLO His daughter is to be brought by you to the supper.
LUCENTIO And then?
BIONDELLO The old priest at Saint Luke's church is at your command
          at all hours.
LUCENTIO And what of all this?
BIONDELLO I cannot tell, except they are busied about a counter-
          feit assurance. Take you assurance of her, 'cum privi-
          legio ad imprimendum solum'.[146] To th'church! Take the
          priest, clerk, and some sufficient honest witnesses.   90
          If this be not that you look for, I have no more to say,
          But bid Bianca farewell for ever and a day.

[*He turns to go.*

LUCENTIO Hear'st thou, Biondello?
BIONDELLO I cannot tarry: I knew a wench married in an after-
          noon as she went to the garden for parsley to stuff a

rabbit; and so may you, sir; and so adieu, sir. My
master hath appointed me to go to Saint Luke's, to bid
the priest be ready to come, against you come with
your appendix.[147]   [*Exit.*

LUCENTIO I may and will, if she be so contented.   100
She will be pleased, then wherefore should I doubt?
Hap what hap may, I'll roundly go about her;
It shall go hard, if Cambio go without her.   [*Exit.*

SCENE 5.

The road to Padua.

Enter PETRUCHIO, KATHERINA, HORTENSIO *and* SERVANTS.

PETRUCHIO Come on, a God's name! Once more toward
our father's.
Good Lord, how bright and goodly shines the moon!
KATHERINA 'The moon'? The sun: it is not moonlight now.
PETRUCHIO I say it is the moon that shines so bright.
KATHERINA I know it is the sun that shines so bright.
PETRUCHIO Now by my mother's son, and that's myself,
It shall be moon, or star, or what I list,
Or ere I journey to your father's house.
[*To the servants:*] Go on, and fetch our horses back again.[148]
– Evermore crossed and crossed, nothing but crossed!   10
HORTENSIO [*to Katherina:*] Say as he says, or we shall never go.
KATHERINA Forward, I pray, since we have come so far,
And be it moon, or sun, or what you please;
And if you please to call it a rush-candle,
Henceforth I vow it shall be so for me.
PETRUCHIO I say it is the moon.
KATHERINA   I know it is the moon.
PETRUCHIO Nay, then you lie: it is the blessèd sun.
KATHERINA Then, God be blessed, it is the blessèd sun;
But sun it is not, when you say it is not,
And the moon changes even as your mind: 20
What you will have it named, even that it is,
And so it shall be so, for Katherine.[149]

HORTENSIO Petruchio, go thy ways: the field is won.

PETRUCHIO Well, forward, forward! Thus the bowl should run,
    And not unluckily against the bias.
    But soft, company is coming here.[150]

Enter VINCENTIO.

    [*To Vincentio:*] Good morrow, gentle mistress; where
                      away?
    – Tell me, sweet Kate, and tell me truly too,
    Hast thou beheld a fresher gentlewoman?
    Such war of white and red within her cheeks!   30
    What stars do spangle heaven with such beauty
    As those two eyes become that heavenly face?
    – Fair lovely maid, once more good day to thee.
    – Sweet Kate, embrace her for her beauty's sake.

HORTENSIO [*aside:*] A will make the man mad, to make a woman
                      of him.

KATHERINA Young budding virgin, fair and fresh and sweet,
    Whither away, or where is thy abode?[151]
    Happy the parents of so fair a child;
    Happier the man whom favourable stars
    Allots thee for his lovely bedfellow!   40

PETRUCHIO Why, how now, Kate? I hope thou art not mad.
    This is a man, old, wrinkled, faded, withered,
    And not a maiden, as thou say'st he is.

KATHERINA Pardon, old father, my mistaking eyes,
    That have been so bedazzled with the sun
    That everything I look on seemeth green.
    Now I perceive thou art a reverend father:
    Pardon, I pray thee, for my mad mistaking.

PETRUCHIO Do, good old grandsire, and withal make known
    Which way thou travellest; if along with us,   50
    We shall be joyful of thy company.

VINCENTIO Fair sir, and you my merry mistress,[152]
    That with your strange encounter much amazed me,
    My name is called Vincentio, my dwelling Pisa,
    And bound I am to Padua, there to visit
    A son of mine, which long I have not seen.

PETRUCHIO What is his name?

VINCENTIO   Lucentio, gentle sir.

PETRUCHIO Happily met; the happier for thy son.
And now by law, as well as reverend age,
I may entitle thee my loving father. 60
The sister to my wife, this gentlewoman,
Thy son by this hath married.[153] Wonder not,
Nor be not grieved: she is of good esteem,
Her dowry wealthy, and of worthy birth;
Beside, so qualified as may beseem
The spouse of any noble gentleman.
Let me embrace with old Vincentio, [*They embrace.*
And wander we to see thy honest son,
Who will of thy arrival be full joyous.

VINCENTIO But is this true? Or is it else your pleasure, 70
Like pleasant travellers, to break a jest
Upon the company you overtake?

HORTENSIO I do assure thee, father, so it is.

PETRUCHIO Come, go along and see the truth hereof,
For our first merriment hath made thee jealous.
[*Exeunt all except Hortensio.*

HORTENSIO Well, Petruchio, this hath put me in heart.
Have to my widow! And if she be fróward,
Then hast thou taught Hortensio to be untóward.
[*Exit.*

ACT 5, SCENE 1.

A street in Padua, outside Lucentio's house.

Enter GREMIO, *alone; then enter* BIONDELLO, LUCENTIO *(as himself)*
and BIANCA.

BIONDELLO Softly and swiftly, sir, for the priest is ready.

LUCENTIO I fly, Biondello; but they may chance to need thee at
home: therefore leave us.   [*Exeunt Lucentio and Bianca.*

BIONDELLO Nay, faith, I'll see the church a'your back,[154] and then
come back to my master's as soon as I can.   [*Exit.*

GREMIO I marvel Cambio comes not all this while.

Enter PETRUCHIO, KATHERINA, VINCENTIO, GRUMIO
and ATTENDANTS.

PETRUCHIO Sir, here's the door: this is Lucentio's house.
My father's bears more toward the market-place;
Thither must I, and here I leave you, sir.

VINCENTIO You shall not choose but drink before you go.
I think I shall command your welcome here,   10
And by all likelihood some cheer is tóward.

                              [*He knocks.*

GREMIO They're busy within, you were best knock louder.

                  [*Vincentio knocks more loudly.*

The PEDANT *looks out of a window above.*

PEDANT What's he that knocks as he would beat down the gate?

VINCENTIO Is Signor Lucentio within, sir?

PEDANT He's within, sir, but not to be spoken withal.

VINCENTIO What if a man bring him a hundred pound or two, to
make merry withal?

PEDANT Keep your hundred pounds to yourself; he shall need
none, so long as I live.

PETRUCHIO [*to Vincentio:*] Nay, I told you your son was well beloved   20
in Padua. [*To pedant:*] Do you hear, sir? – to leave
frivolous circumstances, I pray you tell Signor Lucentio
that his father is come from Pisa, and is here at the door
to speak with him.

PEDANT   Thou liest! His father is come from Mantua[155] and here
           looking out at the window.

VINCENTIO Art thou his father?

PEDANT   Ay sir, so his mother says, if I may believe her.

PETRUCHIO [to Vincentio:] Why, how now, gentleman? Why, this is   30
           flat knavery, to take upon you another man's name.

PEDANT   Lay hands on the villain! I believe a means to cozen
           somebody in this city under my countenance.

                          Enter BIONDELLO.

BIONDELLO [aside:] I have seen them in the church together; God
           send 'em good shipping. But who is here? Mine old
           master, Vincentio! Now we are undone, and brought
           to nothing.

VINCENTIO [to Biondello:] Come hither, crack-hemp.

BIONDELLO I hope I may choose, sir.

VINCENTIO Come hither, you rogue. What, have you forgot me?   40

BIONDELLO Forgot you? No, sir: I could not forget you, for I
           never saw you before in all my life.

VINCENTIO What, you notorious villain, didst thou never see thy
           master's father, Vincentio?[156]

BIONDELLO What, my old, worshipful old master? Yes, marry, sir –
           see where he looks out of the window.

VINCENTIO Is't so, indeed?   [*He beats Biondello.*

BIONDELLO Help, help, help! Here's a madman will murder me!
                                                     [*Exit Biondello.*

PEDANT   Help, son! Help, Signor Baptista!   [*Exit from above.*

PETRUCHIO Prithee, Kate, let's stand aside, and see the end of this   50
           controversy.   [*They stand aside.*

   Enter the PEDANT *(below) with* BAPTISTA, TRANIO *(as Lucentio)*
                        and SERVANTS.

TRANIO   Sir, what are you, that offer to beat my servant?

VINCENTIO What am *I*, sir? Nay, what are *you*, sir? O immortal
           gods! O fine villain! A silken doublet, a velvet hose, a
           scarlet cloak, and a copatain hat! O, I am undone, I am
           undone! While I play the good husband at home, my
           son and my servant spend all at the university.

TRANIO   How now, what's the matter?

BAPTISTA   What, is the man lunatic?

TRANIO   [to Vincentio:] Sir, you seem a sober ancient gentleman   60
            by your habit, but your words show you a madman.
            Why, sir, what 'cerns it you, if I wear pearl and gold? I
            thank my good father, I am able to maintain it.

VINCENTIO   Thy father! O villain, he is a sail-maker in Bergamo![157]

BAPTISTA   You mistake, sir, you mistake, sir. Pray, what do you
            think is his name?

VINCENTIO   His name? As if I knew not his name! I have brought
            him up ever since he was three years old, and his name
            is Tranio.

PEDANT   Away, away, mad ass! His name is Lucentio, and he is   70
            mine only son, and heir to the lands of me, Signor
            Vincentio.

VINCENTIO   'Lucentio'! O, he hath murdered his master! Lay hold
            on him, I charge you, in the Duke's name. O, my
            son, my son![158] Tell me, thou villain, where is my son,
            Lucentio?

TRANIO   Call forth an officer.

                    Enter an OFFICER.

            – Carry this mad knave to the jail. Father Baptista, I
            charge you see that he be forthcoming.

VINCENTIO   Carry me to the jail!   80

GREMIO   Stay, officer: he shall not go to prison.

BAPTISTA   Talk not, Signor Gremio; I say he *shall* go to prison.

GREMIO   Take heed, Signor Baptista, lest you be cony-catched
            in this business; I dare swear this is the right Vincentio.

PEDANT   Swear, if thou dar'st.

GREMIO   Nay, I dare not swear it.

TRANIO   Then thou wert best say that I am not Lucentio.

GREMIO   Yes, I know thee to be Signor Lucentio.

BAPTISTA   Away with the dotard, to the jail with him!

VINCENTIO   Thus strangers may be haled and abused. O monstrous   90
            villain!

                    Enter BIONDELLO, LUCENTIO *and* BIANCA.

BIONDELLO   O, we are spoiled, and yonder he is!
            Deny him, forswear him, or else we are all undone.

LUCENTIO   [kneeling:] Pardon, sweet father.

VINCENTIO   Lives my sweet son?

Exeunt BIONDELLO, TRANIO *and* PEDANT *'as fast as may be'.*[159]

BIANCA   [*kneeling:*] Pardon, dear father.
BAPTISTA   How hast thou offended?
            Where is Lucentio?
LUCENTIO   Here's Lucentio,
            Right son to the right Vincentio,
            That have by marriage made thy daughter mine,
            While counterfeit supposes bleared thine eyne.[160]
GREMIO   Here's packing with a witness, to deceive us all!   100
VINCENTIO   Where is that damnèd villain, Tranio,
            That faced and braved me in this matter so?
BAPTISTA   Why, tell me, is not this my Cambio?
BIANCA   Cambio is changed into Lucentio.
LUCENTIO   Love wrought these miracles. Bianca's love
            Made me exchange my state with Tranio,
            While he did bear my countenance in the town;
            And happily I have arrived at the last
            Unto the wishèd haven of my bliss.
            What Tranio did, myself enforced him to;   110
            Then pardon him, sweet father, for my sake.
VINCENTIO   I'll slit the villain's nose that would have sent me to
            the jail!
BAPTISTA   [*to Lucentio:*] But do you hear, sir? Have you married
            my daughter without asking my good will?
VINCENTIO   Fear not, Baptista; we will content you: go to. But I
            will in, to be revenged for this villainy.
                                                      [*Exit.*
BAPTISTA   And I, to sound the depth of this knavery.
                                                      [*Exit.*
LUCENTIO   Look not pale, Bianca; thy father will not frown.
                                      [*Exeunt Lucentio and Bianca.*
GREMIO   My cake is dough, but I'll in among the rest,   120
            Out of hope of all but my share of the feast.
                                                      [*Exit.*
KATHERINA   Husband, let's follow, to see the end of this ado.
PETRUCHIO   First kiss me, Kate, and we will.
KATHERINA   What, in the midst of the street?
PETRUCHIO   What, art thou ashamed of me?
KATHERINA   No sir, God forbid; but ashamed to kiss.

PETRUCHIO Why, then let's home again. [*To Grumio:*] Come,
                          sirrah, let's away.
KATHERINA Nay, I will give thee a kiss: now pray thee, love, stay.
                             [*They kiss.*
PETRUCHIO Is not this well? Come, my sweet Kate.
        Better once than never, for never too late.[161]   130
                                [*Exeunt.*

SCENE 2.

Inside Lucentio's house.

Enter BAPTISTA *and* VINCENTIO, GREMIO *and the* PEDANT, LUCENTIO
and BIANCA, PETRUCHIO *and* KATHERINA, HORTENSIO *and the*
WIDOW; *then* TRANIO, GRUMIO, BIONDELLO *and other* SERVANTS
bringing in a banquet.[162]

LUCENTIO At last, though long, our jarring notes agree;
        And time it is, when raging war is done,
        To smile at scapes and perils overblown.
        My fair Bianca, bid my father welcome,
        While I with self-same kindness welcome thine.
        Brother Petruchio, sister Katherina,
        And thou, Hortensio, with thy loving widow,
        Feast with the best, and welcome to my house.
        My banquet is to close our stomachs up,
        After our great good cheer.[163] Pray you, sit down,   10
        For now we sit to chat, as well as eat. [*They sit and eat.*
PETRUCHIO Nothing but sit and sit, and eat and eat!
BAPTISTA Padua affords this kindness, son Petruchio.
PETRUCHIO Padua affords nothing but what is kind.
HORTENSIO For both our sakes, I would that word were true.
PETRUCHIO Now, for my life, Hortensio fears his widow.
WIDOW Then never trust me if I be afeard.
PETRUCHIO You are very sensible, and yet you miss my sense:
        I mean, Hortensio is afeard of you.
WIDOW He that is giddy thinks the world turns round.   20
PETRUCHIO Roundly replied.
KATHERINA   Mistress, how mean you that?
WIDOW Thus I conceive by him.[164]

PETRUCHIO Conceives by me! How likes Hortensio that?

HORTENSIO My widow says, thus she conceives her tale.

PETRUCHIO Very well mended. Kiss him for that, good widow.

KATHERINA 'He that is giddy thinks the world turns round':
I pray you, tell me what you meant by that.

WIDOW Your husband, being troubled with a shrew,
Measures my husband's sorrow by his woe:
And now you know my meaning.   30

KATHERINA A very mean meaning.

WIDOW   Right, I mean you.

KATHERINA And I am mean, indeed, respecting you.[165]

PETRUCHIO To her, Kate!

HORTENSIO To her, widow!

PETRUCHIO A hundred marks, my Kate does put her down.

HORTENSIO That's my office.

PETRUCHIO Spoke like an officer; ha' to thee, lad![166]

                              [*He drinks to Hortensio.*

BAPTISTA How likes Gremio these quick-witted folks?

GREMIO Believe me, sir, they butt together well.

BIANCA Head and butt! An hasty-witted body   40
Would say your head and butt were head and horn.

VINCENTIO Ay, mistress bride, hath that awakened you?[167]

BIANCA Ay, but not frighted me; therefore I'll sleep again.

PETRUCHIO Nay, that you shall not: since you have begun,
Have at you for a better jest or two.

BIANCA Am I your bird? I mean to shift my bush,
And then pursue me as you draw your bow.[168]
– You are welcome all.

                    [*Exeunt Bianca, Katherina and the widow.*

PETRUCHIO She hath prevented me. Here, Signor Tranio,
This bird you aimed at, though you hit her not;   50
Therefore a health to all that shot and missed.

TRANIO O sir, Lucentio slipped me like his greyhound,
Which runs himself, and catches for his master.

PETRUCHIO A good swift simile, but something currish.

TRANIO 'Tis well, sir, that you hunted for yourself:
'Tis thought, your deer does hold you at a bay.[169]

BAPTISTA O, O, Petruchio! Tranio hits you now.

LUCENTIO I thank thee for that gird, good Tranio.

HORTENSIO Confess, confess, hath he not hit you here?

PETRUCHIO A has a little galled me, I confess;   60
             And as the jest did glance away from me,
             'Tis ten to one it maimed you two outright.

BAPTISTA Now, in good sadness, son Petruchio,
             I think thou hast the veriest shrew of all.

PETRUCHIO Well, I say no; and therefore, Sir Assurance,[170]
             Let's each one send unto his wife,
             And he whose wife is most obedient
             To come at first when he doth send for her
             Shall win the wager which we will propose.

HORTENSIO Content. What's the wager?

LUCENTIO   Twenty crowns.   70

PETRUCHIO Twenty crowns!
             I'll venture so much of my hawk or hound,
             But twenty times so much upon my wife.

LUCENTIO A hundred then.

HORTENSIO   Content.

PETRUCHIO   A match! 'Tis done.

HORTENSIO Who shall begin?

LUCENTIO   That will I. – Go,
             Biondello, bid your mistress come to me.

BIONDELLO I go.   [Exit.

BAPTISTA Son, I'll be your half, Bianca comes.[171]

LUCENTIO I'll have no halves; I'll bear it all myself.

                   Enter BIONDELLO.

             How now, what news?

BIONDELLO   Sir, my mistress sends you word   80
             That she is busy, and she cannot come.

PETRUCHIO How? 'She's busy, and she cannot come':
             Is that an answer?

GREMIO   Ay, and a kind one too.
             Pray God, sir, your wife send you not a worse.

PETRUCHIO I hope, better.

HORTENSIO Sirrah Biondello, go and entreat my wife
             To come to me forthwith.   [Exit Biondello.

PETRUCHIO   O ho! 'Entreat' her!
             Nay, then she must needs come.

HORTENSIO   I am afraid, sir,

     Do what you can, yours will not be entreated.

             Enter BIONDELLO.

     Now, where's my wife?   90

BIONDELLO She says you have some goodly jest in hand.
     She will not come; she bids you come to her.

PETRUCHIO Worse and worse! 'She will not come'! O vilde,
     Intolerable, not to be endured!
     Sirrah Grumio, go to your mistress:
     Say, I command her come to me.   [*Exit Grumio.*

HORTENSIO I know her answer.

PETRUCHIO   What?

HORTENSIO   She will not.

PETRUCHIO The fouler fortune mine, and there an end.

             Enter KATHERINA.

BAPTISTA Now, by my hollidam, here comes Katherina!

KATHERINA What is your will, sir, that you send for me?   100

PETRUCHIO Where is your sister, and Hortensio's wife?

KATHERINA They sit conferring by the parlour fire.

PETRUCHIO Go fetch them hither; if they deny to come,
     Swinge me them soundly forth unto their husbands.
     Away, I say, and bring them hither straight.

                          [*Exit Katherina.*

LUCENTIO Here is a wonder, if you talk of a wonder.

HORTENSIO And so it is; I wonder what it bodes.

PETRUCHIO Marry, peace it bodes, and love, and quiet life,
     An awful rule, and right supremacy;
     And, to be short, what not, that's sweet and happy?   110

BAPTISTA Now fair befall thee, good Petruchio!
     The wager thou hast won, and I will add
     Unto their losses twenty thousand crowns,
     Another dowry to another daughter,
     For she is changed, as she had never been.

PETRUCHIO Nay, I will win my wager better yet,
     And show more sign of her obedience,
     Her new-built virtue and obedience.

     Enter KATHERINA *with* BIANCA *and the* WIDOW.

     See where she comes, and brings your fróward wives

	As prisoners to her womanly persuasion. 120
	– Katherine, that cap of yours becomes you not:
	Off with that bauble, throw it under-foot! [*She obeys.*
WIDOW	Lord, let me never have a cause to sigh,
	Till I be brought to such a silly pass!
BIANCA	Fie! What a foolish duty call you this?
LUCENTIO	I would your duty were as foolish too:
	The wisdom of your duty, fair Bianca,
	Hath cost me five hundred crowns since
	supper-time.[172]
BIANCA	The more fool you, for laying on my duty.
PETRUCHIO	Katherine, I charge thee, tell these headstrong women 130
	What duty they do owe their lords and husbands.
WIDOW	Come, come, you're mocking; we will have
	no telling.
PETRUCHIO	Come on, I say, and first begin with her.
WIDOW	She shall not.
PETRUCHIO	I say, she shall – and first begin with her.
KATHERINA	[*addressing in turn the widow and Bianca:*]
	Fie, fie! Unknit that threatening unkind brow,
	And dart not scornful glances from those eyes
	To wound thy lord, thy king, thy governor.
	It blots thy beauty as frosts do bite the meads,
	Confounds thy fame as whirlwinds shake fair buds, 140
	And in no sense is meet or amiable.
	A woman moved is like a fountain troubled,
	Muddy, ill-seeming, thick, bereft of beauty;
	And while it is so, none so dry or thirsty
	Will deign to sip or touch one drop of it.
	Thy husband is thy lord, thy life, thy keeper,
	Thy head, thy sovereign;[173] one that cares for thee
	And for thy maintenance; commits his body
	To painful labour, both by sea and land,
	To watch the night in storms, the day in cold, 150
	Whilst thou liest warm at home, secure and safe;
	And craves no other tribute at thy hands
	But love, fair looks and true obedience:
	Too little payment for so great a debt.
	Such duty as the subject owes the prince,

Even such a woman oweth to her husband;
And when she is fróward, peevish, sullen, sour,
And not obedient to his honest will,
What is she but a foul contending rebel
And graceless traitor to her loving lord?   160
I am ashamed that women are so simple,
To offer war where they should kneel for peace,
Or seek for rule, supremacy and sway,
When they are bound to serve, love and obey.[174]
Why are our bodies soft, and weak, and smooth,
Unapt to toil and trouble in the world,
But that our soft conditions and our hearts
Should well agree with our external parts?
Come, come, you fróward and unable worms:
My mind hath been as big as one of yours,   170
My heart as great; my reason haply more,
To bandy word for word and frown for frown;
But now I see our lances are but straws,
Our strength as weak, our weakness past compare:
That seeming to be most, which we indeed least are.
Then vail your stomachs, for it is no boot,
And place your hands below your husband's foot:[175]
In token of which duty, if he please,
My hand is ready: may it do him ease.

PETRUCHIO Why, there's a wench! Come on, and kiss me, Kate.   180
LUCENTIO Well, go thy ways, old lad, for thou shalt ha't.[176]
VINCENTIO 'Tis a good hearing, when children are tóward.
LUCENTIO But a harsh hearing, when women are fróward.
PETRUCHIO Come Kate, we'll to bed.
    We three are married, but you two are sped.
    [*To Lucentio:*] 'Twas I won the wager, though you hit
                    the white,
    And, being a winner, God give you good night![177]
                [*Exeunt Petruchio and Katherina.*
HORTENSIO Now go thy ways; thou hast tamed a curst shrow.[178]
LUCENTIO 'Tis a wonder, by your leave, she will be tamed so.
                           [*Exeunt.*

APPENDIX:
THE 'CHRISTOPHER SLIE' MATERIAL
IN *THE TAMING OF A SHREW*.

The original printed text of Shakespeare's *The Taming of the Shrew* is defective, for the plot of Christopher Sly's deception by a nobleman, which constitutes the Induction and is briefly continued just before Petruchio's arrival, is not sustained and completed. In contrast, the anonymous play entitled *The Taming of a Shrew* does sustain and complete its similar plot concerning the deception of 'Christopher Slie'. Furthermore, *The Taming of a Shrew* appears to derive largely from a lost version of Shakespeare's play in which the complementary Sly material was present. Accordingly, stage productions of *The Taming of the Shrew* often draw on the 'Slie' parts of that anonymous work to augment the Sly story. The extracts which follow are taken from the 1594 text, *A Pleasant Conceited Historie, called The taming of a Shrew*. Some of the spellings, punctuation-conventions and stage-directions have been modernised, and occasionally the lineation has been emended. In scene 2, I expand 'Simeon' as 'See-me-on', to clarify Slie's pun.

[SCENE I.]

Enter a TAPSTER, *beating out of his doors* SLIE, *drunken.*

TAPSTER   You whoreson drunken slave, you had best be gone,
                And empty your drunken paunch somewhere else,
                For in this house thou shalt not rest tonight.
                                              [Exit tapster.
SLIE   Tilly vally! By Chrisee, tapster, I'll fese you anon.
                Fill's the tother pot and all's paid for. Look you,
                I do drink it of mine own instigation; *omne bene.*

Here I'll lie a while; why, tapster, I say,
Fill's a fresh cushen here.
Heigh ho, here's good warm lying.   [*He falls asleep.*

    Enter a LORD *and his* MEN *from hunting.*

LORD   Now that the gloomy shadow of the night,
Longing to view Orion's drizzling looks,
Leaps from th'antarctic world unto the sky
And dims the welkin with her pitchy breath,
And darksome night o'ershades the crystal heavens,
Here break we off our hunting for tonight.
Couple up the hounds and let us hie us home,
And bid the huntsman see them meated well,
For they have all deserved it well today.
– But soft, what sleepy fellow is this lies here?
Or is he dead? See, one, what he doth lack.

SERVANT   My lord, 'tis nothing but a drunken sleep:
His head is too heavy for his body, and he
Hath drunk so much that he can go no furder.

LORD   Fie, how the slavish villain stinks of drink!
– Ho, sirrah, arise! What, so sound asleep?
– Go take him up and bear him to my house
(And bear him easily, for fear he wake),
And in my fairest chamber make a fire,
And set a sumptuous banquet on the board,
And put my richest garments on his back;
Then set him at the table in a chair.
When that is done, against he shall awake,
Let heavenly music play about him still.
Go, two of you, away and bear him hence,
And then I'll tell you what I have devised;
But see, in any case, you wake him not.
                      [*Exeunt two with Slie.*
Now take my cloak and give me one of yours:
All fellows now; and see you take me so,
For we will wait upon this drunken man,
To see his count'nance when he doth awake
And find himself clothèd in such attire,
With heavenly music sounding in his ears,
And such a banquet set before his eyes:

The fellow sure will think he is in heaven.
But we will be about him when he wakes,
And see you call him 'lord' at every word,
And offer thou him his horse to ride abroad,
And thou his hawks, and hounds to hunt the deer,
And I will ask what suits he means to wear;
And, whatsoe'er he saith, see you do not laugh,
But still persuade him that he is a lord.

Enter MESSENGER.

MESSEN.   And it please your Honour, your players be come,
And do attend your Honour's pleasure here.

LORD   The fittest time they could have chosen out!
Bid one or two of them come hither straight.

[*Exit messenger.*

Now will I fit myself accordingly,
For they shall play to him when he awakes.

*Enter two of the players (*SANDER *and* TOM,
with back-packs) and a BOY.

Now sirs, what store of plays have you?

SANDER   Marry, my lord, you may have a tragical
Or a commodity, or what you will.

TOM   'A comedy', thou shouldst say. Souns! Thou'lt shame us
all.

LORD   And what's the name of your comedy?

SANDER   Marry, my lord, 'tis called *The Taming of a Shrew*: 'tis a
good lesson for us, my lord, for us that are married men.

LORD   *The Taming of a Shrew*: that's excellent, sure.
Go see that you make you ready straight,
For you must play before a lord tonight.
Say you are his men and I your fellow.
He's something foolish, but, whatsoe'er he says,
See that you be not dashed out of countenance.
[*To boy:*] And sirrah, go you make you ready straight,
And dress yourself like some lovely lady;
And, when I call, see that you come to me,
For I will say to him thou art his wife.
Dally with him and hug him in thine arms,
And if he desire to go to bed with thee,

Then feign some scuse and say thou wilt anon.
Be gone, I say, and see thou dost it well.

BOY   Fear not, my lord, I'll dandle him well enough,
And make him think I love him mightily.   [*Exit boy.*

LORD   Now, sirs, go you and make you ready too,
For you must play as soon as he doth wake.

SANDER   O brave, sirrah Tom! We must play before
A foolish lord. Come, let's go make us ready.
Go get a dishclout to make clean your shoes,
And I'll speak for the properties. – My lord, we must
Have a shoulder of mutton for a property,
And a little vinegar to make our devil roar.

LORD   Very well. – Sirrah, see that they want nothing.
                                                  [*Exeunt omnes.*

[SCENE 2.]

MUSICIANS *are present. Enter* FOUR SERVANTS, *two bearing a
table with a banquet on it, the other two bearing* SLIE,
who is asleep in a chair and richly apparelled.

SERVANT 1 So. Sirrah, now go call my lord, and tell him that all
           things is ready as he willed it.

SERVANT 2 Set thou some wine upon the board, and then I'll go
           fetch my lord presently.   [*Exit.*

           Enter the LORD (*disguised as 'Simon'*) *and his* MEN.

LORD   How now, what, is all things ready?

SERVANT 1 Ay, my lord.

LORD   Then sound the music, and I'll wake him straight,
           And see you do as erst I gave in charge.   [*Music.*
           – My lord, my lord! – He sleeps soundly. – My lord!

SLIE   Tapster, gi's a little small ale. Heigh-ho.

LORD   Here's wine, my lord, the purest of the grape.

SLIE   For which lord?

LORD   For your Honour, my lord.

SLIE   Who, I? Am I a lord? Jesus, what fine apparel have I got!

LORD   More richer far your Honour hath to wear,
           And, if it please you, I will fetch them straight.

MAN 1   And if your Honour please to ride abroad,
            I'll fetch you lusty steeds more swift of pace
            Than wingèd Pegasus in all his pride,
            That ran so swiftly over the Persian plains.

MAN 2   And if your Honour please to hunt the deer,
            Your hounds stands ready coupled at the door,
            Who, in running, will o'ertake the roe
            And make the long-breath'd tiger broken-winded.

SLIE   By the Mass, I think I am a lord indeed!
            What's thy name?

LORD   Simon, and it please your Honour.

SLIE   'Simon': that's as much to say 'Simeon – See-me-on',
            or 'Simon put forth thy hand and fill the pot'. Give me
            thy hand, Sim. Am I a lord indeed?

LORD   Ay, my gracious lord; and your lovely lady
            Long time hath mournèd for your absence here;
            And now with joy behold where she doth come
            To gratulate your Honour's safe return.

Enter BOY *in woman's attire.*

SLIE   Sim, is this she?

LORD   Ay, my lord.

SLIE   Mass, 'tis a pretty wench; what's her name?

BOY   Oh, that my lovely lord would once vouchsafe
            To look on me, and leave these frantic fits,
            Or were I now but half so eloquent
            To paint in words what I'll perform in deeds,
            I know your Honour then would pity me.

SLIE   Hark you, mistress: will you eat a piece of bread?
            Come sit down on my knee. – Sim, drink to her, Sim,
            For she and I will go to bed anon.

LORD   May it please you, your Honour's players be come
            To offer your Honour a play.

SLIE   A play, Sim! O brave! Be they my players?

LORD   Ay, my lord.

SLIE   Is there not a Fool in the play?

LORD   Yes, my lord.

SLIE   When will they play, Sim?

LORD   Even when it please your Honour: they be ready.

BOY	My lord, I'll go bid them begin their play.
SLIE	Do, but look that you come again.
BOY	I warrant you, my lord, I will not leave you thus.

                                        [*Exit boy.*

SLIE	Come, Sim, where be the players? Sim, stand by me and we'll flout the players out of their coats.
LORD	I'll call them, my lord. – Ho! Where are you there?

                                    [*Trumpets sound.*

. . .

[End of SCENE 5.]

SLIE	Sim, when will the Fool come again?
LORD	He'll come again, my lord, anon.
SLIE	Gi's some more drink here! – Souns, where's the tap-ster? – Here, Sim, eat some of these things.
LORD	So I do, my lord.
SLIE	Here, Sim, I drink to thee.
LORD	My lord, here comes the players again.
SLIE	O, brave! Here's two fine gentlewomen.

. . .

[End of SCENE 14.]

SLIE	Sim, must they be married now?
LORD	Ay, my lord.

[SCENE 15.]

Enter FERANDO, KATE *and* SANDER.

SLIE	Look, Sim, the Fool is come again now.

. . .

[Middle of SCENE 16.]

PHYLOTUS *and* VALERIA *run away.*

SLIE	I say we'll have no sending to prison.
LORD	My lord, this is but the play: they're but in jest.
SLIE	I tell thee, Sim, we'll have no sending to prison, that's

flat. Why, Sim, am not I Don Christo Vary?
Therefore I say they shall not go to prison.

LORD   No more they shall not, my lord: they be run away.

SLIE   Are they run away, Sim? That's well.
Then gi's some more drink, and let them play again.

LORD   Here, my Lord.   [Slie drinks and then falls asleep.

. . .

[Near the end of SCENE 16.]

                                   [Slie sleeps.

LORD   Who's within there?

                   Enter BOY and SERVANTS.

                          Come hither, sirs: my lord's
Asleep again. Go take him easily up
And put him in his own apparel again,
And lay him in the place where we did find him,
Just underneath the alehouse side below.
But see you wake him not, in any case.

BOY   It shall be done, my lord. – Come, help to bear him
                                        hence.
                                   [Exeunt.

. . .

[SCENE 19.]

Enter TWO SERVANTS bearing SLIE (who is wearing his original
apparel). The servants leave Slie where they found him, and go out.

                   Enter the TAPSTER.

TAPSTER   Now that the darksome night is overpast
And dawning day appears in crystal sky,
Now must I haste abroad. But soft, who's this?
What, Slie? Oh wondrous! Hath he lain here all night?
I'll wake him. I think he's starved by this,
But that his belly was so stuffed with ale.
What ho, Slie! Awake, for shame!

SLIE   Sim, gi's some more wine. What, 's all the players
gone: am not I a lord?

TAPSTER   A lord with a murrin! Come, art thou drunken still?

SLIE   Who's this? Tapster? Oh Lord, sirrah, I have had
            The bravest dream tonight that ever thou
            Heardest in all thy life.

TAPSTER   Ay, marry, but you had best get you home,
            For your wife will course you for dreaming here tonight.

SLIE   Will she? I know now how to tame a shrew.
            I dreamt upon it all this night till now;
            And thou hast waked me out of the best dream
            That ever I had in my life.
            But I'll to my wife presently,
            And tame her, too, and if she anger me.

TAPSTER   Nay, tarry, Slie, for I'll go home with thee
            And hear the rest that thou hast dreamt tonight.

                                              [*Exeunt.*

                        FINIS

NOTES ON *THE TAMING OF THE SHREW*

In these notes, the abbreviations include the following:

c.	*circa* (Latin): approximately;
Cf., cf.:	*confer* (Latin): compare;
e.g.:	*exempli gratia* (Latin): for example;
F1:	the First Folio (1623);
F2:	the Second Folio (1632);
i.e.:	*id est*: that is;
O.E.D.:	*The Oxford English Dictionary* (2nd edition, 1989, and website);
S.D.:	stage-direction;
S.P.:	speech-prefix.

Biblical quotations are from the Geneva Bible (1560).

In the case of a pun or an ambiguity, the meanings are distinguished as (a) and (b), or as (a), (b) and (c).

1 (title) SHREW: The word means 'cantankerous person'. Shakespeare rhymes 'shrew' with 'show', 'woe' and 'so'.

2 (Ind.1.4) *Richard Conqueror;*: Sly's drunken error for 'William the Conqueror'.

3 (Ind.1.7) *Go . . . Jeronimie;*: Sly confuses Hieronimo in Thomas Kyd's play *The Spanish Tragedie* (who says 'Not I, *Hieronimo* beware, goe by, goe by.') with St Jerome.

4 (Ind.1.9–11) *thirdborough . . . law.*: In F1, the hostess says 'Headborough' (constable), but the emendation to 'thirdborough' (also meaning 'constable') is required by Sly's response.

5 (Ind.1.14–17) *Breathe . . . fault?*: 'Breathe' is an emendation of F1's 'Brach'; while 'embossed', 'brach' and 'in the coldest fault' mean 'beaded with sweat', 'bitch' and 'when the scent was almost lost'.

6 (Ind.1.61) w*hen . . . is,*:   i.e. 'when he says that he remains mad,'. Some editors emend it as 'when he says he is Sly,' (although the lord does not know Sly's name).

7 (Ind.1.80–85) *This . . . means.*:   'Soto' ('a farmer's eldest son') is a character in John Fletcher's *Women Pleas'd* (*c.* 1620) and presumably in an earlier play on which Fletcher's is based. (Incidentally, *Women Pleas'd* says that women desire above all 'to have their will'.) As Soto does not 'woo' a gentlewoman, line 84 probably refers to a rôle taken by Player 1. F1's S.P. for line 85 is '*Sincklo*', John Sincklo being an actor with the King's Men.

8 (Ind.1.96) *If . . . impatient.*:   The line scans as pentameter if 'impatient' is pronounced tetrasyllabically ('im-páy-see-ènt').

9 (Ind.2.S.D.) *Enter, aloft . . . LORD.*:   The S.D. in F1 is: '*Enter aloft the drunkard with attendants, some with apparel, Bason and Ewer, & other appurtenances, & Lord.*' The subsequent F1 speech-prefixes ('*1.Ser.*', '*2.Ser.*', etc.,) define the attendants as servants. The fictional location is a room in the lord's house, but the intended theatrical location is evidently an upper stage or large gallery. Scholars question the feasibility of such staging.

10 (Ind.2.17–21) *Burton-Heath . . . not::*   Barton-on-the-Heath and Wilmcote ('Wincot') are villages about fourteen miles (22.5 km.) and three miles (4.8 km.) respectively from the centre of Stratford-upon-Avon, and in 1591 a Hacket family lived in or near Wilmcote.

11 (Ind.2.33–7) *Apollo . . . Semiramis.*:   Apollo is the classical god of music, and Semiramis was a legendary (and notoriously lustful) Assyrian queen.

12 (Ind.2.48–51) *Adonis . . . wind.*:   Adonis was the legendary beautiful youth loved by Cytherea (Venus).

13 (Ind.2.52–4) *Io . . . done.*:   Ovid's *Metamorphoses* (Book 1, lines 588–600) says that Jupiter raped the virgin Io after telling her she would be safe in a forest and then casting darkness over the region. (Some editors sustain the metre of line 53 by marking the 'ed' of 'beguiled' as a sounded syllable, but the word may be pronounced trisyllabically – 'be-*guy*-uld' – without this expedient.)

14 (Ind.2.55–8) *Daphne . . . drawn.*:   Ovid's *Metamorphoses* (Bk.1, 490–552) tells how Apollo pursued the virgin Daphne to rape her, but she eluded him by being transformed into a laurel tree.

(During the chase, Apollo feared that brambles would scratch her limbs.)

15 (Ind.2.61) *waning age*.:   Ovid's *Metamorphoses* and Spenser's *Faerie Queene* helped to propagate the notion of a general decline from a pristine 'Golden Age' to the present state of humankind.

16 (Ind.2.85–6) *And say . . . quarts*.:   A 'leet' is a local court, and a 'sealed quart' is an officially-marked quart measure. (Sly has alleged that the hostess gives short measure.)

17 (Ind.2.91) *Greece,*:   'Greece' may be a misreading of 'Greet', the name of a village in Gloucestershire.

18 (Ind.2.119–20) *I hope . . . long;*: The Page says 'stands', meaning 'suffices'; Sly indicates that his penis 'stands so' (i.e., 'is so largely erect') that he could only with difficulty wait a long time for her.

19 (Ind.2.125–8) *For . . . play*:   Attending a play was (like singing and dancing) one of the recommended therapies for melancholy, which was believed to thicken the blood and possibly induce madness.

20 (1.1.25) Perdonatemi,:   F1 has '*Me Pardonato,*'. Some editors emend this as '*Mi perdonate,*' but that is the incorrect second person plural indicative. '*Perdonatemi,*' though metrically less smooth, offers the correct second person plural imperative: 'Pardon me (sir),'.

21 (1.1.31–3) *Let's . . . abjured*.: 'let us be neither Stoics (philosophers advocating restraint) nor stocks (blockheads), I pray, nor people so devoted to Aristotle's counsels of moderation as to render Ovid (poetic advocate of sexual pleasure) a rejected outcast.'

22 (1.1.S.D. after line 47) *[Lucentio . . . Bianca).*:   In F1, the equivalent S.D. is: '*Enter Baptista with his two daughters, Katerina & Bianca, Gremio a Pantelowne, Hortensio sister to Bianca. Lucen. Tranio, stand by.*' A 'pantaloon' ('*Pantelowne*') is a stock type, the foolish old man, in the Italian *commedia dell'arte*. The error '*sister*' (for '*suitor*') indicates the unreliability of F1.

23 (1.1.57–8) *is . . . mates?*:   'is it your desire to make a laughing-stock of me among these male companions?' 'Stale' could also mean 'prostitute' and 'cat's-paw', and her phrasing suggests 'stalemate' (deadlock) in chess. In lines 59–60, Hortensio interprets 'mates' as 'husbands'.

24 (1.1.62) *Iwis . . . heart;*: 'Certainly, marriage is not even a half-hearted interest of hers;'. (Her use of the third person to refer to herself is perhaps meant to emphasise her detachment.)

25 (1.1.66) *From . . . us!*: During the Litany, as specified in the Anglican *Booke of Common Prayer*, 1584, the priest says 'from all the deceites of the world, the flesh and the deuill', and the congregation responds 'Good Lord deliuer vs' [i.e. 'deliver us'].

26 (1.1.78–9) *A pretty . . . why.*: 'A pretty pet! The best thing she could do would be to weep – if she could find a pretext.' (Here, as at 1.1.128, 1.2.16 and elsewhere, 'and' means 'if'.)

27 (1.1.85) *Signor Baptista,*: F1 generally renders as 'Signior' the correct vocative form 'Signor' or 'signor' ('Mr').

28 (1.1.103–4) *What . . . Ha!*: In F1, the line-breaks come after 'though' and 'take,'. The present re-arrangement yields one line of hexameter and one of pentameter (though with a feminine ending). Some editors set the lines as prose.

29 (1.1.107–9) *Their . . . sides.*: 'Love bestowed by women is not so important, Hortensio, as to prevent our waiting patiently and managing equably without it. We have both failed in our plans.' Although 'Their love' matches F1, some editors emend the phrase as 'There; love'.

30 (1.1.138–9) *Happy . . . ring.*: Proverbs: 'Happy man be his dole' means 'May happiness be allotted to the winner', while 'He that runs the fastest gets the ring' means 'The best contestant deserves the prize'.

31 (1.1.152) *As Anna . . . was::* Dido, Queen of Carthage, loved Æneas, and Anna was her sister and confidante. (See Virgil's *Æneid*, Bk. 4, and Marlowe's *Dido, Queen of Carthage*.)

32 (1.1.153–6) *Tranio . . . wilt.*: In these three lines, Lucentio employs the rhetorical figures of epanalepsis (when the same word begins and ends a line), asyndeton (phrases accumulated without intervening conjunctions), ploce (repetition) and parison (structural duplication).

33 (1.1.160) *'Redime . . . minimo.'*: 'Ransom yourself from captivity as cheaply as you can': advice (from Terence's play *Eunuchus*) which Shakespeare had seen quoted in the '*Ablatus post verbum*' section of William Lily's *Latin Grammar*.

34 (1.1.166–8) *Such . . . strand.*: Ovid's *Metamorphoses* (Bk. 2, 846–75) tells how Jupiter (Jove), in the form of a bull, carried

Europa (daughter of Agenor) away on his back from Sidon towards Crete. It was actually in Sidon that Jupiter 'humble[d] him to her hand'.

35 (1.1.182) *Because . . . suitors.*:   'because then she will not be troubled by suitors.' Some editors emend F1's 'she' to 'he'.

36 (1.1.220–22) *Where . . . news?*:   F1 prints these lines (and lines 236–41) as prose.

37 (1.1.232) *I . . . whit.*:   F1 has 'I sir, ne're a whit.', which means either (a) 'I sir? Not in the least.' or (b) 'Ay (yes) sir – not at all.'.

38 (1.1.S.D. after 245) *The . . . speak.*:   F1 has: '*The Presenters aboue speakes.*' (The combination of plural noun and singular verb is not unusual in Elizabethan drama.) As the 'presenter' of the main play is the lord, and the subsequent speakers include a servant, I term the speakers here 'observers' rather than 'presenters'.

39 (1.1.S.D. after 251) *[They . . . observe.*:   F1 has: '*They sit and marke.*' In *The Taming of the Shrew*, the observers do not speak again; whereas, in *The Taming of a Shrew*, they do speak again, and the Sly (or Slie) plot is concluded at the play's end. See 'Appendix: the "Christopher Slie" Material'.

40 (1.2.S.D.) PETRUCHIO: Shakespeare often anglicised foreign names. 'Petruchio', from the Italian 'Petruccio' (meaning 'Peterkin'), was then probably pronounced 'Pet-*roo*-chee-oh' by the playwright. (Similarly, 'Lucentio' and 'Vincentio' were probably pronounced 'Loo-*sen*-tee-oh' and 'Vin-*sen*-tee-oh'.)

41 (1.2.8) *knock me here soundly.*:   'knock vigorously here for me'. Petruchio uses 'me' as an 'ethic dative', a colloquial device which means sometimes 'for me' and sometimes 'I tell you'. Grumio takes it to be grammatically accusative.

42 (1.2.16–S.D.) *Faith . . . down.*:   'Ring' puns on ringing (a doorbell) and wringing (a neck or ear). To '*sol-fa*' is to sing the notes of a musical scale (and, here, to cry out in pain). In George Gascoigne's play *Supposes* (one of the sources of *The Taming of the Shrew*), Psiteria threatens Crapine thus: 'If I come neere you hempstring, I will teache you to sing sol fa.' F1's S.D. is: '*He rings him by the eares*'. In my version, '*forcing him down*' is an inference from line 27's 'Rise, Grumio, rise'.

43 (1.2.18) *Help . . . help!*:   F1 has 'Helpe mistris helpe,'. Many editors substitute 'masters' for 'mistris' (i.e. 'mistress'). In 5.1.5, F1 gives 'mistris' where 'master's' makes more sense.

44 (1.2.24–6) *Con . . . Petruccio.*:   The Italian means 'With all
   my heart, well met' (i.e. 'Most cordial greetings') and 'Welcome to our house, my most honoured Mr Petruchio.' These
   Italian characters kindly revert to English, and Grumio even
   claims that Petruchio has uttered Latin.

45 (1.2.32) *two . . . out?*:   This is probably an allusion to the card-
   game 'One-and-Thirty', of which the aim was to collect
   thirty-one 'pips' (spots on the cards). Thus 'a pip out' may
   mean 'in error', 'awry' or 'slightly crazy'. ('Two-and-thirty'
   could also mean 'drunk'.)

46 (1.2.50) *Where . . . few.*:   F1 has 'Where small experience
   growes but in a few.', meaning 'Only in a few people does
   experience, initially limited, grow.' Some editors emend the
   line as 'Where small experience grows. But in a few,' – the last
   part meaning 'But, to speak briefly,'.

47 (1.2.67–71) *Be she . . . rough*:   John Gower's *Confessio Amantis*,
   Bk. 1, 1407–1861, gives the tale of Florent (i.e. Florentius), a
   knight who marries an ugly old woman in exchange for her
   life-saving secret (though, in bed, she then becomes a beautiful
   young woman). Ovid's *Metamorphoses*, Bk.14, 132–53, says that
   Apollo granted the Cumaean Sibyl (a prophetess) as many
   years of life as there were grains of sand in a heap nearby; but
   she forgot to ask for youth, and would have to undergo
   centuries of old age. Xanthippe (here 'Zentippe', as in F1) was
   the shrewish wife of the philosopher Socrates. F2 substitutes
   'time. Were she' for F1's 'me. Were she is'.

48 (1.2.109–13) *rail . . . cat.*:   Here 'rail in his rope-tricks' probably means 'abuse her in showy rhetoric'; 'throw a figure in her
   face' means 'assail her with a figure of speech'; and 'no more
   eyes . . . than a cat' may refer to the saying 'Well might the cat
   wink when both her eyes were out'.

49 (1.2.S.D. after 136) *Enter . . . schoolmaster.*:   F1's S.D., '*Enter
   Gremio and Lucentio disguised.*', is placed after the present line 134.
   Nevertheless, Grumio's remarks, from 'Here's no knavery!' to
   'heads together. –', appear to be partly-sarcastic comments on
   the scheme hatched by Hortensio and Petruchio. He does not
   yet know about the scheme of Lucentio and Gremio. The S.D.
   is therefore better located between lines 136 and 137.

50 (1.2.150) *To whom . . . her?*:   The F1 line is: 'To whom they

go to: what will you reade to her.' Deletion of the second 'to' improves the grammar and the metre.

51 (1.2.187–8) *Antonio's . . . me,*: 'Antonio's' emends F1's '*Butonios*'. Some editors emend F1's 'my fortune' as 'his fortune', but 'my fortune lives for me' (i.e., 'my wealth is now solely at my disposal') makes sufficient sense.

52 (1.2.194) *Will . . . her.*: He recalls the proverb, 'Wedding and hanging go by destiny.'

53 (1.2.210) *yours.*: Some editors emend to 'ours.', but perhaps Gremio is seeking to shift any expense on to Hortensio.

54 (1.2.220–22) *Hark . . . pray.*: Line 220 appears in F1 as 'Hearke you sir, you meane not her to —— '. The sense, metre and rhyme-scheme are improved if the dash is replaced by 'woo'. The 'her' is Bianca, though the ambiguous phrasing of lines 218–21 leads Petruchio (in line 222) to seek confirmation. Tranio's 'Perhaps him and her' means 'I may woo her and win her father over'. 'What have you to do?' means 'What business is it of yours?'.

55 (1.2.239–42) *Fair . . . alone.*: 'Fair Leda's daughter' was Helen (wife of Menelaus), who eloped with Paris, the Trojan prince. In Ovid's *Heroides*, Bk. 17, 103–4, she says she had a thousand suitors.

56 (1.2.252–3) *leave . . . twelve.*: Hercules (also called Alcides), whose strength was legendary, undertook twelve great 'labours' (tasks).

57 (1.2.262) *feat,*: F1 has 'seeke,'. The compositor probably misread the handwriting. (At line 271, F1 offers 'contriue' instead of 'convive'.)

58 (1.2.267) *benvenuto.*: 'welcome.' Hortensio means that he will pay Petruchio's bill.

59 (2.1.S.D.) *her clothing . . . tied,*: The torn clothing and tied hands (not specified in F1's S.D.) are editorial inferences from the dialogue, but such later directions as '*strikes her*' and '*She rushes at Bianca*' derive from F1's '*Strikes her*' and '*Flies after Bianca*'.

60 (2.1.3) *goods,*: F1 has 'goods,' meaning 'possessions,' but many editors emend it to 'gauds,' or 'gawds,' meaning 'baubles, playthings,'.

61 (2.1.33–4) *I must . . . hell.*: Sometimes an unmarried older

sister danced bare-foot at a sister's wedding. Proverbially, unmarried women ('old maids') after death led apes in hell, perhaps because they had no children to lead them into heaven.

62 (2.1.S.D. after 38) Enter . . . books).:   In F1, the S.D. is defective: 'Enter Gremio, Lucentio, in the habit of a meane man, Petruchio with Tranio, with his boy bearing a Lute and Bookes.' F1 elsewhere spells the musician's name variously as 'Litio' and 'Lisio', indicating anglicised pronunciation ('Liss-ee-oh') of the Italian name 'Licio'. F2 uses the spellings 'Litio' and 'Licio', the latter being the correct Italian form deriving from the Roman 'Lucius'.

63 (2.1.73) Backare!:   Trisyllabic mock-Latin meaning 'Move back!'. F1 prints 71–3 as prose and 76–87 as verse.

64 (2.1.141) That . . . not,:   Another instance of a singular verb with a plural noun (see also 2.1.348 and 4.5.40). While F1 has 'That shakes not,' F2 (partly clarifying the sense) has 'That shake not,'.

65 (2.1.S.D. after 141) 'Enter . . . broke.':   I quote the excellent S.D. of F1. Line 156 suggests that he may be wearing the smashed lute round his neck, though in Act 3, scene 1, his lute is evidently tunable.

66 (2.1.149) frets,:   Here 'frets' means 'ridges (on the lute's finger-board) to aid fingering'. At line 152, Kate exploits another sense of 'frets': 'vexations'.

67 (2.1.189) (For . . . cates),:   F1 has 'For dainties are all Kates,'. There is a homophonic pun: 'cates' (meaning 'delicacies'), 'Kates' and 'Kate's'. (At 2.1.271, in contrast, 'Kates' appears to rhyme with 'cats'. The pronunciation varied.)

68 (2.1.194–7) Myself . . . movable.:   By 'moved', he means 'emotionally inclined', but she takes it to mean 'transported by somebody, like a "movable" (a piece of furniture)'. The phrase 'in good time!' means 'indeed!'.

69 (2.1.206–8) 'Should . . . buzzard.:   Petruchio's 'buzz!' is the sound of the bee which he punningly elicits from 'be', and 'buzz!' was also an exclamation of impatience. Her reply means: 'Well caught – though by chance rather than skill, as by a buzzard (which cannot be trained for falconry).' Petruchio then asks: 'O, slowly-moving turtle-dove (symbol of faithful love), will this buzzard (Petruchio) capture you?' Her obscure

retort means perhaps that she should be recognised only as a dove of a predatory kind which can take (swallow) a cock-chafer or similar buzzing insect (this being another meaning of 'buzzard'): in other words, he won't capture her, but she will defeat him.

70 (2.1.215–16) *Yours . . . arms.*:   In line 215, 'tales' means (a) 'stories, rumours' (e.g. that she is 'light', i.e. promiscuous), and (b) tails, i.e. fundaments or pudenda: hence his bawdy question in line 216. The subsequent S.D. is an inference from lines 219 and 235. Similarly, the S.D. at 245 is an inference from the ensuing dialogue.

71 (2.1.219–22) *So . . . books!*:   'Lose' connotes both 'loosen' and 'be deprived of '. She implies: (a) in order to cuff her, he will loosen his grip on her; (b) he may lose his arms as a punishment for ill-treating her; and (c) he may be deprived of his coat of arms for behaving in an ungentlemanly manner. He responds that if she is skilled in heraldry, she could register him as a gentleman (and regard him with favour).

72 (2.1.223–7) *What . . . crab.*:   A 'crest' is (a) a heraldic device and (b) the 'comb' or tuft on a bird's head. A 'coxcomb' is (a) the comb of a cock and (b) the Fool's cap. A 'combless cock' is a submissive cock (in a sexual sense, too), and a 'craven' is an unsuccessful or cowardly fighting-cock. A 'crab' is a sour crab-apple.

73 (2.1.252–5) *Did . . . sportful!*:   Diana, the woodland huntress, was the classical goddess of chastity.

74 (2.1.259) *Yes . . . warm.*:   Kate alludes to the proverb 'He is wise enough that can keep himself warm': in other words, Petruchio's wisdom is minimal.

75 (2.1.270–71) *wild . . . Kates.*:   Here 'wild Kate' puns on 'wild-cat', and 'household Kates' suggests 'domestic cats'.

76 (2.1.288–9) *For . . . chastity;*:   'Grissell' or Patient Griselda (famously depicted in Chaucer's 'The Clerk's Tale') was a model of patient obedience. 'Roman Lucrece' or Lucretia (the subject of Shakespeare's *The Rape of Lucrece*) was a model of wifely chastity.

77 (2.1.317) *kiss . . . Sunday'.*:   'We will be married o' Sunday' is, with variants, the refrain of several ballads. ('I mun be married a Sunday' is sung in Udall's comedy, *Ralph Roister*

Doister, written *c.* 1552.) Whether Petruchio and Kate kiss here or not is a matter of critical or directorial opinion, the original S.D. being simply '*Exit Petruchio and Katherine.*'.

78 (2.1.319–24) *Faith . . . catch.*: Baptista says that he is like a merchant who gambles madly in a hopeless market. Tranio comments that the merchandise was deteriorating (and fretting with vexation), and now it will either bring profit or be a disastrous loss. Baptista says that the only profit he seeks is to see Kate quietly married. Gremio sarcastically remarks that Petruchio has, no doubt, gained a quiet bride.

79 (2.1.337) *Shall . . . love.*: F2 deletes the 'my'. Baptista's promise in lines 335–7 seems to contradict his view (expressed with regard to Kate in line 129) that the woman's love was the crucial consideration.

80 (2.1.393–6) *Sirrah . . . boy.*: 'Young fellow, young gambler, your father would be a fool to give you everything he has and to live on your charity in his declining years. Ha, that's a joke, a piece of nonsense! A crafty old Italian is not so benevolent, my lad.'

81 (2.1.398) *I have . . . ten.*: 'I have bluffed my way with a low-valued card.' His proverbial claim apparently derives from the card-game 'Primero'.

82 (3.1.1) *Fiddler . . . sir!*: Perhaps 'Licio' has taken Bianca's hand, ostensibly to teach her the lute's fingering.

83 (3.1.4) *But . . . is*: The line is incomplete. Editors have suggested such emendations as: 'But, wrangling pedant, this Urania is' (Urania being a muse of cosmic harmony); 'But, wrangling pedant, this Bianca is'; and 'She is a shrew, but, wrangling pedant, this is'.

84 (3.1.28–9) '*Hic . . . senis.*': 'Here ran the Simois [a river]; here is the Sigeian land [the plain of Troy]; here stood the lofty palace of old Priam.' (Ovid, *Heroides*, 1, 33–4.)

85 (3.1.36) *old pantaloon.*: 'ridiculous old man', another allusion to the stock comic character in the *commedia dell'arte*. Oddly, Lucentio talks as though his only rival is Gremio, even though he knows that Hortensio, too, is a rival.

86 (3.1.50–51) *Æacides . . . grandfather.*: Ovid's *Heroides*, 1, 35, refers to Æacides, meaning 'descendant of Æacus', here one of his grandsons: possibly Ajax, probably Achilles, both being

legendary warriors.

87 (3.1.46–56) *How . . . both.*: F1 allocates lines 46–9 to Lucentio, 50–51 to Bianca, and 52–6 to Hortensio.

88 (3.1.65) *gamouth*: In this scene, F1 spells the word as 'gamouth' four times and 'gamoth' once. Editors often emend it as 'gamut', the modern term. It refers to the musical scale as established by Guido d'Arezzo, in which the first note of a hexachord (group of six notes) bears the same name. (Line 71 refers to that musical note.)

89 (3.1.72–6) '"A re", . . . die.': *A re, B mi*, etc., are the subsequent notes in the gamut. Where two hexachords overlap, each note has two names, so that D is note 5 (*sol*) in the G hexachord and note 2 (*re*) of the C hexachord.

90 (3.2.11) *wooed . . . leisure.*: a variant of the proverb 'Marry in haste, and repent at leisure'.

91 (3.2.16) *Make . . . banes,*: F1 has 'Make friends, inuite, and proclaime the banes,' which is metrically and logically defective. Editorial emendations vary. One is: 'Make feast, invite friends, and proclaim the banns,'. By keeping 'banes', I preserve the Shakespearian pronunciation.

92 (3.2.28–9) *For such . . . humour.*: I follow the text of F1, though this yields two irregular lines, the first being either passably hexametrical (with six iambic metrical feet) or clumsily pentametrical (if 'injury' be read as 'inj'ry'), the second being awkwardly defective. F2 regularises the lines by deleting 'very' from the first of them and adding 'thy' ('of thy impatient humour') to the second.

93 (3.2.30–31) *such old . . . of!*: F1 lacks 'old' (meaning 'plentiful'), which is required by the responses in lines 32 and 40.

94 (3.2.75–80) *Why . . . many.*: Baptista says 'Why, that's all one', meaning 'But that's the same'. Biondello retorts with a jingle containing the offer to bet a penny (with St James as authority and witness) that a horse plus a man are more than one – but not much more (implying that a man is worth little).

95 (3.2.85) *Were . . . thus?*: i.e. 'Was it not better for me to hasten here, even if dressed like this?'. F1 has 'Were it better I should rush in thus:', which, being metrically and logically defective, solicits emendation.

96 (3.2.112–14) *Could . . . myself.*: There is probably a bawdy

allusion: 'what she will wear in me' may mean 'the part of me that she will wear out (i.e. the penis)'.

97 (3.2.122) *But . . . add*:   F1 has 'But sir, Loue concerneth vs to adde', which editors variously emend. The transition from line 121 to 122 is peculiar. At 118–20, Tranio was going to help persuade Petruchio to change his clothes, yet at 122 he remains behind (instead of following Petruchio) and is responding to an unheard speech by Lucentio. Between 121 and 122, therefore, a scene, or part of a scene, may be missing, particularly as little time is left for Petruchio to take Katherina to church and marry her. Some editors begin a new scene (Act 3, scene 3) after the present line 121.

98 (3.2.134) *'Twere . . . marriage,*:   In the phrase 'steal our marriage' (meaning 'elope and marry secretly'), 'marriage' can be pronounced trisyllabically to preserve the metre.

99 (3.2.160) *What . . . again?*:   This follows F1. F2 emends the line as 'What said the wench when he rose up againe?'. Some editors prefer: 'What said the vicar when he rose again?'.

100 (3.2.161–77) *Trembled . . . play.*:   These lines were set as prose in F1 but corrected to verse in F2.

101 (3.2.199) *the oats . . . horses.*:   Grumio is perhaps mocking the weak and sick state of the horses. (In line 198, 'horse' may be plural.)

102 (3.2.204) *You . . . green.*:   'Trot off while your boots are new.'

103 (3.2.209–10) *I will . . . leisure.*:   'I will be angry if it suits me; what right have you to interfere? – Father, don't say anything; he shall wait until I am ready.'

104 (3.2.225) *My . . . anything;*:   The tenth commandment (Exodus 20:17, Geneva Bible) says: 'Thou shalt not couet thy neighbours house, nether shalt thou couet thy neighbours wife, nor his man seruant, nor his maid, nor his oxe, nor his asse, nether any thing that is thy neighbours.'

105 (4.1.5) *a little . . . hot,*:   proverbial, meaning 'a small person soon becomes angry'.

106 (4.1.16–17) *fire . . . water.*:   He quotes and adapts a round of the 'Scotland's Burning' (or 'London's Burning') type, which includes (with variants) the refrain 'Fire, fire! Fire, fire! Cast on water! Cast on water!'.

107 (4.1.20) *winter . . . beast:* :   An allusion to the proverb, 'Age

(or winter) and wedlock tame both man and beast.'

108   (4.1.24–5) *thy horn . . . least.*:   'the horn projecting from your head (denoting that you are a cuckold and resemble a beast) is a foot in length – and my penis is at least as long.'

109   (4.1.36–7) *Why . . . thou.*:   He quotes another round, which begins (with variations): 'Jack boy, ho boy! News'. The clause 'The devil is dead' is found in several songs of that time. F1 has 'wilt thou'; F2 has 'thou wilt'.

110   (4.1.42–4) *the white . . . without,*:   Some editors emend 'the white' as 'their white'. 'Jacks' were (a) leather drinking-vessels and (b) male servants; 'Jills' were (a) vessels, usually metal, with a capacity of one gill, and (b) female servants.

111   (4.1.57) *'tis . . . tale;*:   Grumio exploits the ambiguity of 'sensible', which means (a) 'capable of being felt' (from the Latin *sentire*, to feel), (b) 'rational', (c) 'striking', and (d) 'markedly painful' (*O.E.D.*).

112   (4.1.82–3) *kiss . . . hands.*:   i.e. kiss their own hands as a mark of respect to their master.

113   (4.1.86–93) *You . . . them.*:   The dialogue exploits the ambiguity of 'countenance' and 'credit'. The former term can mean (a) 'pay respects to' and (b) 'provide a face for'; while the latter term can mean (a) 'honour' and (b) 'provide credit for'.

114   (4.1.S.D. after 93) *Enter . . . GREGORY*:   The S.D. in F1 is: '*Enter foure or fiue seruingmen.*', but (apart from the name of Gregory, whose presence may be implied in the response to Petruchio's question at line 108) their names are provided by speech-prefixes.

115   (4.1.105) *Where . . . door:*   This line follows F1, but some editors make the last phrase 'at the door', in order to improve the metre.

116   (4.1.114) *malt-horse drudge!*:   menial toiler like a heavy horse used on a treadmill where malted barley is ground.

117   (4.1.125–6) *'Where . . . those'–*:   He sings part of a ballad which, like that begun at line 130, is now lost.

118   (4.1.127) *Food . . . food!*:   Numerous editors thus emend F1's 'Soud, soud, soud, soud.', but some editors follow F1, speculating that 'soud' may be an interjection of impatience.

119   (4.1.S.D. after 132) *[He . . . servant.*:   This, like numerous

other stage-directions, is an inference from the dialogue.

120 (4.1.167–72) *In . . . hither!*:   F1 sets these lines as prose.

121 (4.1.183) *Last . . . not,*:   No night has yet elapsed since the wedding, unless a night was spent on the journey (which usually takes about five hours, according to Petruchio at 4.3.182–3).

122 (4.1.196) *Now . . . speak*::   In the Marriage Service, as specified in *The Booke of Common Prayer* (1584), the priest says that if any man knows of any lawful objection to the marriage, 'let him nowe speake'.

123 (4.2.8) *The . . . Love.*:   Ovid's *Ars Amatoria*, a Latin guide to seduction.

124 (4.2.22–3) *I have . . . Bianca.*:   In Act 1, scene 2, Hortensio told Tranio (as 'Lucentio') that Bianca was 'the chosen of Signor Hortensio'; but, in Act 2, scene 1, Tranio seemed to be unaware of Hortensio's suit.

125 (4.2.35) *Would . . . forsworn!*:   'I wish that everyone except Cambio had rejected her' (presumably because Hortensio thinks that Bianca would never be allowed to marry a mere tutor).

126 (4.2.57) *tricks . . . long,*:   'tricks which are exactly right': another reference to the card-game 'One-and-Thirty', in which the aim was to acquire a hand of thirty-one points.

127 (4.2.63) *a marcantant . . . pedant,*:   F1's 'marcantant' is a version of the then-obsolete Italian *mercatante*, meaning 'merchant'. (The modern noun *mercante* was already current.) Although some of the later allusions (e.g., at 4.2.89–90 and 97–8) suggest that this old man is a merchant, stage-directions and speech-prefixes in F1 identify him as 'Pedant' (i.e., a teacher or tutor).

128 (4.2.71) *Take . . . alone.*:   F1 reads: 'Take me your loue, and then let me alone.', and attributes this line to a mysterious '*Par.*'.

129 (4.2.120) *Go . . . you.*:   To improve the metre, F2 emends the line as 'Goe with me sir to cloath you as becomes you.'

130 (4.3.2) *The more . . . appears.*:   'The more he wrongs me, the more spiteful he becomes.'

131 (4.3.S.D. after 40) *[He . . . hungrily.*:   This S.D., not in F1, is an inference from the dialogue, as is the S.D. after 43.

132 (4.3.43) *all . . . proof.*:   'all my efforts are in vain.'

133 (4.3.91) *Like . . . shop;*:   A censer ('Censor' in F1) was a

fumigator, a perforated incense-burner. (Barbers would not only cut hair but also singe it, and would sometimes let blood as a supposed therapy for various ailments.) Some editors emend 'Censor' as 'scissor'.

134   (4.3.112) *As . . . liv'st!*:   'that you will remember your foolish talk as long as you live.'

135   (4.3.121–4) *Thou . . . braved.*:   Grumio puns on 'faced', meaning 'trimmed' and 'defied', and on 'braved', meaning 'adorned' and 'defied or challenged'.

136   (4.3.130–33) *Imprimis . . . gown.*:   'Imprimis' is Latin for 'First'. Grumio denies the term 'loose-bodied gown', as the garment was associated with 'loose' women. A 'bottom' is a spool or core.

137   (4.3.145–8) *And . . . me.*:   The tailor says: 'If I had you in a suitable place (for fighting), you would acknowledge the truth.' Grumio replies: 'I am ready for you now: use the order-note as your weapon, give me your yard-measure as mine, and attack me as well as you can.'

138   (4.3.152–4) *take . . . use!*:   Petruchio means: 'Take it away, so that your master can use it as he wishes.' Grumio reproaches the tailor, bawdily imputing to him the wish to lift up Katherina's gown for the master's sexual pleasure.

139   (4.3.176–7) *If . . . forthwith,*:   'If it seems disgraceful to you, blame me; and, accordingly, joyfully, we will proceed immediately,'. Some editors treat 'frolic' not as an adverb or adjective but as a verb: 'If it seems disgraceful to you, blame me, and accordingly rejoice. We will proceed immediately,'.

140   (4.3.182–5) *Let's . . . there.*:   Dinner-time was around noon, supper-time around 7 p.m.

141   (4.4.S.D.) *Enter . . . Vincentio).*:   In F1, the S.D. is: '*Enter Tranio, and the Pedant drest like Vincentio.*' 18 lines later, F1 has: '*Enter Baptista and Lucentio: Pedant booted and bare headed.*': perhaps the scene originally opened there.

142   (4.4.5) *Where . . . Pegasus.*:   F1 makes this the first line of Tranio's response. 'Pegasus' (the name of the classical flying horse) was also the name of various inns in Shakespeare's London. It is quite possible that Genoan inns included a 'Pegaso'.

143   (4.4.52) *Pitchers . . . servants;*:   He recalls the proverb, 'Small

pitchers have wide ears' (i.e., 'Subordinates may overhear'), a pitcher's 'ears' being its handles.

144 (4.4.S.D. after 58) *[He . . . him.*: This S.D. is not in F1, but the wink is specified at line 74.

145 (4.4.S.D. after 68) *Enter . . . servant.*: In F1, the S.D. is '*Enter Peter.*', though he never speaks; perhaps the script was cut. (A different Peter was one of Petruchio's servants.) Some editors begin a new scene (Act 4, scene 5) after the present line 72.

146 (4.4.88–9) '*cum . . . solum*'.: This Latin inscription, often taken to mean 'with the exclusive right to print', appeared in many books. Here 'print' implies 'imprinting one's likeness, fathering a child'.

147 (4.4.98–9) *to come . . . appendix*.: Some editors emend F1's 'to come' as 't'attend'. '[A]gainst you come' means 'in readiness for your arrival', and 'appendix' here means 'appendage (bride-to-be)'.

148 (4.5.9) *Go . . . again.*: The implication may be that the travellers have been walking to give their horses a rest. (Horses were not normally employed in the Elizabethan theatre.)

149 (4.5.22) *And . . . Katherine.*: F1 has: 'And so it shall be so for *Katherine.*' (i.e. 'and consequently, that is how it shall be, where Katherine is concerned.'); but some editors emend 'be so' to 'be, sir,' or 'be still,'.

150 (4.5.26) *But . . . here.*: Some editors emend this metrically-defective line as 'But soft, what company is coming here?' or 'But soft, some company is coming here.'.

151 (4.5.35–7) *A will . . . abode?*: In line 35, F2 emends as 'a woman' F1's 'the woman'. In 37, F1 has 'Whether away, or whether is thy abode?', but F2 corrects 'or whether' to 'or where'.

152 (4.5.52) *Fair . . . mistress,*: To improve the metre, the final word can be pronounced trisyllabically ('*miss*-ter-ess').

153 (4.5.61–2) *The sister . . . married.*: This event has not yet occurred; but, at line 73, Hortensio confirms Petruchio's claim. Hortensio seems to have forgotten that 'Lucentio' (actually Tranio) had sworn never to marry Bianca (4.2.32–3).

154 (5.1.4) *I'll . . . back,*: Probably: 'I'll see the church at your

back,': i.e. 'I'll see you safely married,'.

155 (5.1.26) *from Mantua*:   F1 has 'from Padua', which must be wrong. Editorial suggestions include 'to Padua'; but 'from Mantua' aptly echoes the 'from Pisa' in line 24.

156 (5.1.44) *master's . . . Vincentio?*:   F1 has 'Mistris father, Vincentio?'.

157 (5.1.64) *sail-maker in Bergamo!*:   Though Bergamo is inland, sails were reputedly made there. It was traditionally the home of the harlequin, the comical servant in the *commedia dell'arte*.

158 (5.1.74–5) *O . . . son!*:   Cf. 'ô Absalóm, my sonne, my sonne' (2 Samuel 18:33, Geneva).

159 (5.1.S.D. after 94) *Exeunt . . . be'.*:   F1 has '*Exit Biondello, Tranio and Pedant as fast as may be.*'

160 (5.1.99) *While . . . eyne.*:   'while deceptive suppositions blurred your sight.' ('Eyne', an archaic word for 'eyes', facilitates the rhyme.) The line is a reminder of the importance of George Gascoigne's play *Supposes* as a source of Shakespeare's play. Indeed, this scene of recognition has clear precedent in *Supposes*.

161 (5.1.130) *Better . . . late.*:   Petruchio incompletely blends two proverbs, 'Better late than never' and 'It is never too late to mend'. He means that he and Katherina at last have an established relationship as lovers.

162 (5.2.S.D.) *Enter . . . banquet.*:   F1 calls this scene '*Actus Quintus*' (i.e. 'Act Five'), and the S.D. in F1 is faulty and incomplete: '*Enter Baptista, Vincentio, Gremio, the Pedant, Lucentio, and Bianca. Tranio, Biondello Grumio, and Widdow. The Seruingmen with Tranio bringing in a Banquet.*' (A 'banquet' was often a dessert of fruit, confectionery, wine, etc., following the main meal.) Oddly, Petruchio and Katherina are here obliged to return to the stage immediately after having left it; so possibly there was originally a 'Christopher Sly' episode between what have become scenes 1 and 2 of Act 5.

163 (5.2.8–10) *Feast . . . cheer.*:   'Feast with the best' means 'feed on the best', and 'close our stomachs up' means 'make us replete'. The 'great good cheer', the main part of the feast, would have been at Baptista's house.

164 (5.2.14–22) *Padua . . . him.*:   Petruchio says that Padua provides only what is 'kind', i.e. hospitable. Hortensio, taking

'kind' to mean affectionate, says he hopes that both he and
Petruchio (being newly married) will find that claim true.
Petruchio jestingly suggests that Hortensio fears that the
widow, his wife, will not be affectionate. She, taking 'fears his
widow' to mean 'frightens his bride, the widow', says that she
is assuredly not frightened. Petruchio comments that though
she is judicious, she has misunderstood his meaning, which is
that Hortensio is afraid of her. She retorts that a giddy person
thinks the world is spinning – Petruchio must be naturally
fearful. 'Roundly replied' means 'boldly answered', but carries
the suggestion of 'answered by a rotund person'. 'Thus I
conceive by him' means 'That's my understanding of his
words' but can also mean 'This is how I am, made pregnant
by him': hence Petruchio's apparently shocked response,
'Conceives by me!'.

165 (5.2.31–2) *A very . . . you.*:   Katherina comments that that is a
very ignominious meaning. The widow says that it is natural,
since she refers to Katherina. Katherina's 'I am mean . . .
respecting you' is ambiguous: it suggests (a) 'I can be petty . . .
where you are concerned', (b) 'I am demeaned . . . by the
comparison with you', and possibly (c) 'I am moderate . . .
compared with you'.

166 (5.2.35–7) *A hundred . . . lad!*:   Petruchio says he will bet a
hundred marks that, in the quarrel, Kate will 'put down'
(defeat) the widow. Hortensio responds that it is his own duty
to 'put down' the widow (i.e., have sexual intercourse with
her). Petruchio's 'an officer' means (a) 'a worthy official' and
(b) 'a person experienced in that duty'.

167 (5.2.39–42) *Believe . . . you?*:   Line 39 is rendered by F1 as
'Beleeue me sir, they But together well.' Some editors emend
this as 'Believe me, they butt heads together well.', to cue the
response in line 40. Bianca's reference to 'head and horn' is a
suggestion that the men resemble butting cattle in wearing
horns, theirs being the cuckolds' horns which supposedly
sprout from the heads of betrayed husbands. Vincentio then
asks whether such horny talk (or the horn, i.e. penis) has
aroused her.

168 (5.2.45–7) *Have . . . bow.*:   Some editors emend F1's 'better
iest' as 'bitter jest'. Bianca says that if she resembles a bird, she

will change her location, so that the fowler will not have an easy target.

169 (5.2.56) *your . . . bay.*:   Tranio's 'deer' puns on 'dear'. He suggests that, like a stag at bay, defying its pursuers, Katherina may be holding Petruchio off.

170 (5.2.65) *Sir Assurance,*:   F1 has 'sir assurance,' presumably meaning 'you cocksure fellow,' but some editors emend it as 'for assurance,'.

171 (5.2.75–8) *Who . . . comes.*:   My emendation of F1 (placing ' – Go,' at the end of line 75, whereas F1 has 'Goe' at the start of the next line) patches thus the metre of 75: 'Whó shall begín? Thát will Í. – Gó.'. Some editors emend line 78 by expanding 'I'll' ('Ile' in F1) to 'I will', though the metre is already regular enough if 'I'll' is pronounced disyllabically (here, but not in 79), or if Biondello's 'I go' is added to the line. Baptista means that he will pay half the bet that Bianca will come.

172 (5.2.128) *Hath . . . supper-time.*:   I follow F1's 'Hath cost me fiue hundred crownes since supper time.' Some editors emend the first part as 'Hath cost one hundred crowns' or 'Hath cost me a hundred crowns', to tally with Lucentio's wager at line 74. If, however, Petruchio's bet at lines 71–3 is 400 crowns, and Lucentio's 'A hundred then' means 'I'll raise you a hundred', F1's figure is correct.

173 (5.2.146–7) *Thy . . . sovereign;*:   Biblical teachings: see Genesis 3:16, Ephesians 5:22, and 1 Peter 3:1.

174 (5.2.164) *When . . . obey.*:   The Marriage Service in *The Booke of Common Prayer* (1584) includes this question for the bride: 'Wilt thou obey him, and serue him, loue, honour, and keepe him in sickenesse and in health . . . ?'.

175 (5.2.175–7) *That . . . foot:*:   Line 175 means: 'we seem to be in the greatest degree what we really are in the least degree.': i.e., 'seeming to be the strongest, we are really the weakest.' In line 176, 'vail your stomachs' means 'suppress your pride'; 'it is no boot' means 'there is no reward (for remaining stubborn)'; and putting hands beneath one's husband's foot was evidently a symbolic act of submission and support.

176 (5.2.180–81) *Why . . . ha't.*:   The phrase 'thou shalt ha't' ('you shall have it') means perhaps 'you shall collect your

prize' or, more vaguely, 'you will prevail'; and 'ha't' (here probably pronounced 'hate') rhymes with 'Kate'.

177 (5.2.185–7) *We . . . night!*: 'All three of us are married, but you two (Lucentio and Hortensio) are losers. I won the bet, in effect hitting the pin at the centre of an archer's target, although Lucentio hit the white circle around the pin (since "Bianca" means "White"); and, as I'm the winner, I can now, in prudently departing, magnanimously invoke God's blessing on your nuptial night.'

178 (5.2.188) *shrow*: To guarantee a rhyme with 'so', I preserve the spelling of F1.

GLOSSARY

This glossary serves not only *The Taming of the Shrew* but also the appended material from *The Taming of a Shrew*. Where a pun or an ambiguity occurs, the meanings are distinguished as (a) and (b), or (a), (b) and (c), etc. Otherwise, alternative meanings are distinguished as (i) and (ii), or as (i), (ii) and (iii), etc. Abbreviations include the following: adj., adjective; adv., adverb; App., Appendix; conj., conjunction; Fr., French; Ind., Induction; It., Italian; *O.E.D.*, *Oxford English Dictionary*; Sp., Spanish; vb., verb.

a (as pronoun): 4.5.35, 5.1.32, 5.2.60: he.

a (as preposition): in; **a devil's name**: in the devil's name; **a God's name**: in God's name.

a': **a'my word**: on my word; **a'your back**: at your back.

accord: concord, harmony.

action on: 3.2.227: lawsuit against.

adieu: farewell.

ado: fuss, embroilment.

Adonis: beautiful youth loved by Venus.

advice: **upon advice**: on reflection.

Æacides: descendant of Æacus: e.g. Achilles or Ajax, the legendary warriors.

afeard: afraid.

affect: like; **affected**: 1.1.26: inclined.

affied: betrothed, engaged.

affords: 5.2.13: (a) offers; (b) can afford.

against: **against he shall awake**: in preparation for his awakening; **against you come**: in preparation for your arrival.

Agenor: the father of Europa.

aglet-baby: (perhaps) small carved ornamental figure.

alarum: (i: 1.1.127:) outcry, uproar; (ii: 1.2.203:) call to arms.

Alcides: Hercules.

all one: just the same.

'Amen': 'So be it'.

amort: 4.3.36: (a) sick to death; (b) dispirited.

ancient: 1.2.45: long-standing; **ancient angel**: honest old person.

and (as subordinating conj., e.g. at 1.1.79, 128, 129, 1.2.16, 106, 109, 110, 4.3.145, 4.4.55, etc.): if.

Anna: sister and friend of Queen Dido.

anon: very soon.

answerable to this portion: aptly proportionate.

antic: **veriest antic**: greatest buffoon.

Apollo: Greek god of music.

appendix: appendage: partner.

apply: pursue.

approved: **well approved**: reliable.

argosy: big mercantile ship.

Aristotle: philosopher who advocated moderation.

Arras counterpoints: counterpanes woven at Arras.

assurance: 4.4.88: legal settlement; **take . . . assurance**: make sure.

awful: awe-inspiring.

backare (mock-Latin): back off.

bade: told, directed.

bags: 1.2.174: money-bags.

balk logic: chop logic.

balm (vb.): wash.

banes: banns: public announcements of an intended marriage.

banquet: dessert with fruit and wine.

bar in law: legal impediment.

base: 3.1.45: low, vile.

basta (It.): enough.

bate and beat: flap and flutter.

bauble: trivial item of finery.

bay: **holds you at a bay**: holds you off.

bear (vb.): 2.1.199-202: (a) carry burdens; (b) bear children; (c) bear a man's weight; **bears me fair in hand**: leads me on well.

bear-herd: man who keeps a bear.

beastly: grossly.

beck: nod.

become: 4.5.32: beautify; **as becomes**: as is fitting.

beetle: mallet; **beetle-headed**: wooden-headed.

begnawn with: chewed by.

belike: probably.

be-mete: 4.3.111: (a) beat; (b) measure.

bemoiled: covered in mud.

Bentivolii: Bentivogli, a powerful family in Bologna.

benvenuto (It.): welcome.

beseem: befit.

bespeak: order.

bestraught: distraught.

Bianca: 'White (Pure) Female'.

bias: 4.5.25: (a) weight in a lawn-bowl; (b) curving course of a bowl.

bill: 4.3.141: specification.

bit: mouthpiece.

blot (vb.) sully, disfigure.

blow our nails: wait patiently.

board (vb.): woo.

bondmaid: female slave.

boot: **no boot**: fruitless.

boot-hose: long thick stocking.

bots: worms or maggots.

bottom: spool, core.

brach: bitch.

brave (noun): defiance.

brave (adj.), **bravely** (adv.): handsomely-clad.

braved: (i: 4.3.109; 5.1.102:) defied; (ii: 4.3.123-4: a) adorned; (b) defied.

brav'ry: fine clothes.

braves: 3.1.15: insults, defiances.

break: 2.1.147-8: (a) train; (b) smash.

breathe: give breathing-space to.

breeching: 3.1.18: (a) in breeches: young; (b) liable to be birched.

broiled: grilled.

brooked parle: permitted negotiation.

buckler (vb.): shield.

bug: bugbear, hobgoblin.

burst: broken.

burthen: burden; 1.2.66:
(a) musical accompaniment;
(b) one motive.

but I: 3.1.60; 4.4.2: unless I.

butt: 5.2.39: butt heads together: spar.

buttery: kitchen store-room.

cake's dough, cake is dough:
attempt is a failure.

candle-cases: bags for candle-ends.

caparisoned: equipped.

card-maker: maker of metal combs for wool, hemp, etc.

carouses: **quaff carouses**: drink toasts.

carpets: 4.1.44: (probably) table-cloths.

cart (vb.): send away in a cart.

cates: 2.1.189: (a) delicacies; (b) Kates; (c) Kate's.

censer: fumigator.

'cerns: concerns.

chafe: irritate.

chance: **heavy chance**: sad incident.

chapeless: 3.2.45: (i) with no scabbard; (ii) with incomplete scabbard.

chattels: personal property.

cheer (noun): (i: Ind.2.98; 3.2.181, 5.1.12:) food and/or drink; (ii: 4.3.37: a) state of health; (b) food.

choler: choleric 'humour' (fluid), source of anger;
choleric: causing bile and thus anger.

clapped up: hastily arranged.

clear: 2.1.172: bright.

close (adv.): secretly.

cock: **combless cock**: 2.1.224:
(a) docile male fowl;
(b) compliant penis.

cockle: cockle-shell.

Cock's passion: 4.1.104: God's suffering.

commanded: Ind.1.122: forced.

commodity: item for trade.

comonty: (error for) comedy.

company: **for company**:
together amicably.

compassed: of circular cut.

compound: settle, resolve.

conceive: (i: 5.2.22: a) learn;
(b) become pregnant;
(ii: 5.2.24:) interpret.

conditions: 5.2.167:
characteristics.

confer: converse; **conference**:
conversation.

cony-catched: tricked; **cony-catching**: trickery.

conserves: candied fruits;
conserves of beef: salted beef.

conster: construe.

continency: sexual abstinence.

convive: be convivial.

copatain hat: high conical hat.

countenance (noun): (i: 4.2.65:)
manner; (ii: 4.4.18:) face;
(iii: 5.1.33, 107:) name,
identity; **count'nance**:
(i: 1.1.226: a) bearing;
(b) position; (ii: 4.2.100) face;
dashed out of countenance:
suddenly disconcerted.

countenance (vb.): 4.1.87-92:
(a) pay respects to; (b) provide a face for.

counterpoints: counterpanes.

course: (i: Ind.2.45:) hunt; (ii: 1.1.9:) programme; (iii: App.19:) thrash.

coxcomb: 2.1.223: (a) cock's crest; (b) Fool's cap.

cozen: cheat.

crab: 2.1.227: (a) crab-apple; (b) sour person.

crack (vb.): 1.2.94: explode.

crack-hemp: rogue for hanging.

craven: cowardly male fowl.

credit (noun): reputation.

credit (vb.): 4.1.92-3: (a) honour; (b) provide credit for.

crest: 2.1.223: (a) heraldic device; (b) head-topping.

cried upon it: Ind.1.20: barked to indicate a trail.

cross (vb.): (2.1.28: a:) annoy; (b) contradict; (ii: 4.3.188; 4.5.10:) contradict.

crupper: strap from horse's saddle to its tail.

cullion: testicle: vile man.

cunning: clever, knowledgeable.

curious: 4.4.36: (a) distrustful; (b) niggling; **curiously**: painstakingly.

currish: 5.2.54: (a) cur-like; (b) crude.

curst: cantankerous.

cushen: cuskin: drinking-pot.

custard-coffin: pastry case for custard.

Cytherea: Venus, beautiful goddess of love.

dam: mother.

dame: madam, woman.

dandle: play with.

Daphne: maiden pursued by the god Apollo.

deep-mouthed: deeply-baying.

deer: 5.2.56: (a) deer; (b) dear.

demi-cannon: large cannon-barrel.

denier: Fr. coin of low value.

despiteful: cruel.

Dian: Diana, goddess of chastity.

diaper: cloth, towel.

dinner-time: around noon.

dishclout: dishcloth.

disquiet: disturbed.

dissemble: lie, cheat.

doff: remove.

dole (noun): lot, reward.

domineer: feast riotously.

dotard: old fool.

doublet: tight jacket.

dough: **cake's dough**: project has failed.

ducat: European gold coin.

dulcet: sweet.

dumps: **in your dumps**: depressed.

duty: **have thy duty**: earn your reward.

ears: 4.4.52: handles.

easily: gently.

embossed: beaded with sweat.

entertainment: 2.1.54: reception.

entire: 4.2.23: unalloyed.

entrance to: 2.1.54: entrance-fee for.

ergo (Latin): therefore.

erst: previously.

esteemed him: Ind.1.119: deemed himself.

Europa: princess impregnated by Zeus or Jove.

event: outcome.

execute: 1.1.243: undertake.

exeunt: they go out.

exit: he or she goes out.

extempore: impromptu.

eyne: eyes.

faced: (i: 4.3.121-3: a) trimmed;
(b) outfaced, defied;
(ii: 5.1.102:) outfaced.

fardingales: farthingales:
hooped petticoats.

fare (vb.): Ind.2.97-8: (a)
progress; (b) feed and drink.

fashions: 3.2.49: farcins: con-
tagious disease causing sores.

fault: **in the coldest fault**: when
the scent was almost lost.

fay: faith.

fear (vb.): 5.2.16-17: (a) fear;
(b) frighten; **fear boys with
bugs**: frighten boys with
hobgoblins.

feeze, fese: beat.

fie!: disgusting!, shame on you!;
fie: 3.2.94: for shame; **fie on**:
curse.

fill's: 'fill for us': fill for me.

finis (Latin): the end.

fits: **frantic fits**: bouts of
insanity.

fives: swelling of glands below
the ears.

fleet (adj.): swift.

Florentius: knight who married
a hag.

flourish (noun): fanfare.

flout (vb.): mock.

fool to: 3.2.151: meekly naïve
person in comparison to.

footboy: young male servant.

for: 1.1.88; 3.2.64: instead of.

formal: punctilious.

forsooth: truly.

forswear: renounce.

forthcoming: held for trial.

forward: eager.

fret: 2.1.152: (a) ridge on the
fingerboard of a lute;
(b) vexation.

frolic (adv.): joyfully.

froward: wilful, perverse.

fume (vb.): be angry.

furder: further.

furniture: outfit.

fustian: coarse cloth.

galled: grazed.

galley: long, low-built ship.

galliass: cargo vessel larger than
a galley.

gambold: gambol, frolic.

gamesome: playful.

gamester: gambler.

gamouth: gamut: (a: 3.1.65, 69,
70:) musical scale; (b: 3.1.71:)
lowest note in the scale.

gentles: ladies and gentlemen.

gird (noun): taunt.

girth: saddle-strap passing under
belly.

gi's: 'give us': give me.

glanders: disease causing
swellings beneath the jaw.

God-a-mercy: may God have
mercy.

Gog's wouns: God's wounds.

good-man: husband.

good-night our part: goodbye
to our hopes.

go to: 5.1.116: (a) carry on;
(b) don't worry.

grace: **do me grace**: do me a
favour.

graceless: ungracious.

gramercies (from Fr.): many thanks.

grateful: 2.1.77: gratifying.

gratify: 1.2.258: reward.

gratulate: rejoice at.

green: 4.5.46: fresh, young.

Grissell: Griselda, the legendary patient wife.

groom: rough fellow.

habiliments: clothes.

habit: outfit.

haggard (noun): wild hawk.

haled: dragged.

half: **be your half**: pay half your bet; **half-cheeked**: side-piece faulty.

halt (vb.): limp.

hand: **at any hand**: on any account.

hap (noun): 1.2.264: luck.

hap (vb.): 4.4.102: befall.

haply: perhaps; Ind.1.133: (a) fortunately; (b) perhaps.

happily: (i: 1.2.54: a) fortunately; (b) perhaps; (ii: 4.4.54:) perhaps.

hard: **goes hard**: is serious.

ha' to thee: I drink to thee.

have to: 4.5.77: I'll set about; **have to't afresh**: we'll contest again.

head: **give him head**: let him proceed freely.

head-stall: head-strapping.

hearing: **a good hearing**: good to hear.

heavy: sad; **heavy chance**: sad incident.

Hercules: hero who completed twelve arduous tasks.

hie: hasten.

high cross: stone cross at town centre.

hilding: wretch.

hipped: lame.

hold: (i: 2.1.146:) remain intact; (ii: 3.2.77:) bet.

hollidam: **by my hollidam**: by all I hold sacred.

honest: honourable.

hope: **out of hope of all**: with no hope of anything.

horn: 5.2.41-2: (a) animal's horn; (b) cuckold's horn; (c) penis.

hose: male garment resembling tights.

how now . . . ?: what's this . . . ?

humour: mood; **idle humour**: foolish attitude; **humour of forty fancies**: (obscure, but) some elaborately fanciful ornament; **odd humour**: strange fancy.

hungerly: sparsely.

hurly: tumult.

husband: 5.1.56: housekeeper; **husbanded**: managed.

ill-favoured: unpleasant-looking.

import: **occasion of import**: important event.

imprimis (Latin): first.

indifferent: 4.1.80: (a) matching; (b) unobtrusive.

ingenious: 'befitting a well-born person' (*O.E.D.*).

ingrate: ungrateful.

Io: maiden raped by Jove.

iwis: certainly.

Jack: (i: 2.1.158, 281:) low fellow; (ii: 4.1.43: a) leather drinking-vessel; (b) male servant.

jade: worn-out horse; **prove a jade**: soon tire.

jealous: 4.5.75: sceptical, suspicious.

jerkin: short jacket.

Jeronimie: **Saint Jeronimie**: (confusion of) St Jerome and Kyd's Hieronimo.

Jill: 4.1.44: (a) metal drinking vessel; (b) female servant.

joint-stool: stool made by a joiner.

jointure: provision for a wife's widowhood.

jolly: 3.2.207: (a) very (*O.E.D.*); (b) arrogant.

jolthead: (perhaps) blockhead.

Jove: Jupiter, the supreme Roman deity.

jump in one: coincide.

junkets: sweet delicacies.

Kated: afflicted (as with a disease) with 'the Kate'.

kennel: gutter.

kersey: coarse woollen cloth.

kind: 5.2.14: (a) natural; (b) affectionate; **kindly**: Ind.1.63: (a) naturally; (b) convincingly.

kindness: 5.2.13: natural hospitality.

kite: hawk.

knack: knick-knack

knave: (i: Ind.2.22; 1.2.108; 3.1.45, 47; 5.1.78:) rogue; (ii: 1.2.12; 4.1.142: a) serving-lad; (b) rogue; (iii: 4.1.105, 112, 116:) serving-lad.

knav'ry: folly, nonsense.

lampass: disease of the mouth.

largess: bonus, gift.

'larum: call to arms on trumpet and drum.

lave: wash.

laying: 5.2.129: betting.

Leda: mother of Helen of Troy.

leet: manorial court.

'leges: alleges.

lewd and filthy: cheap and nasty.

lief: **as lief**: as willingly.

lies in's throat: is utterly false.

light (adj.): 2.1.203-4: (a) light in weight; (b) frivolous; (c) quick.

lighted well on: happily discovered.

lightness: fickleness.

link (noun): blacking from a pitch torch.

list (noun): strip of cloth.

list (vb.): please.

logger-headed: wooden-headed, stupid.

longly: persistently.

loss: **merest loss**: Ind.1.20: utter loss (of scent).

love-in-idleness: 1.1.149: (a) the pansy, deemed aphrodisiac; (b) love born of idleness.

lovely: 3.2.118: loving.

Lucrece: Lucretia, the legendary chaste wife.

lure: feathery decoy used to attract a hawk.

lusty: spirited.

maid: virgin, young woman.

make love: woo.

malt-horse drudge: menial toiler, like a heavy horse used on a treadmill.

man my haggard: tame my wild hawk.

marcantant (It. *mercatante*): merchant.

Marcellus' road: anchorage outside Marseille's harbour.

mark (noun): coin or sum of large value.

mark (vb.): notice.

marry: by St Mary.

mart: **desperate mart**: dangerously risky market.

masquing-stuff: showy clothes as for a masque.

Mass: **by the Mass**: By the service of the Holy Eucharist.

me: Ind.1.47; 1.2.8, 11, 12; 4.3.98; 5.2.104: for me.

meacock: meek.

mead: meadow.

mean (adj.): 5.2.32: (a) petty; (b) demeaned; (c) moderate; **mean meaning**: ignominious meaning.

meat: food.

meet (adj.): fitting.

mend . . . with a largess: improve . . . with a bonus.

merest loss: Ind.1.20: utter loss (of scent).

mess: dish of food.

mete-yard: three-foot measure.

methinks: I think.

mew her up: cage her.

milch-kine: cows yielding milk.

mind: 1.1.246: heed, follow.

Minerva: Roman goddess of wisdom.

minion: spoilt darling.

modesty: moderation; **modesties**: restraint.

monument: 3.2.89: portent.

moralise: interpret.

mose in the chine: (perhaps) display final symptoms of glanders.

mother-wit: 2.1.257-8: (a) innate intelligence; (b) mother's intelligence.

movable: piece of furniture.

move: 1.2.70: trouble; **moved**: (i: 2.1.194:) emotionally inclined; (ii: 2.1.195:) transported; (iii: 5.2.142:) exasperated.

mum: be silent.

murrin: murrain: plague.

muscadel: sweet white wine.

nail: length of 2.5 inches (6.3 cm.); **blow our nails**: wait patiently.

near-legged before: (perhaps) knock-kneed in the forelegs.

neat (noun): ox or calf.

nice: 3.1.78: capricious.

nit: 4.3.108: (a) gnat; (b) small fly; (c) louse-egg.

noddle: head.

notorious: exceptional.

odds: 4.3.149: (a) advantage; (b) scraps of material.

of: 5.2.72: on.

offer: 5.1.52: venture.

officer: 5.2.37: (a) worthy official; (b) person experienced in a duty.

old: 3.2.30–32: (a) plentiful; (b) old.

omne bene (Latin): all is well.

omnes (Latin): all.

one: **all one**: the same.

ordnance: **great ordnance**: cannon.

or ere: before.

o' Sunday: on Sunday.

ourselves: of ourselves: by
  nature.

out-vied: out-bidden.

overblown: passed away.

Ovid: Roman author of love-
  poetry.

packing: plotting.

pack-thread: string.

pail: to the pail: supplying the
  dairy and not calves.

pantaloon: ridiculous old man.

Paris: lover of Helen of Troy.

parle: negotiation.

passing (adv.): exceedingly.

passion: merry passion: fit of
  merriment.

paucas pallabris: version of
  pocas palabras (Sp.): few words.

peasant swain: uncouth
  servant.

peat: pet, spoilt child.

pedant: teacher.

pedascule: little teacher.

Pegasus: mythical winged
  horse.

perdonatemi (It.): pardon me.

pieced: mended.

pillory: wooden frame to grip a
  captive's head and arms.

pith of all: main issue.

pittance: meal.

place where: a suitable place.

plash: 1.1.23: (a) pool;
  (b) puddle.

plate: 2.1.340: utensils,
  originally of silver or gold.

pledge (noun): surety, bail.

poesy: poetry.

points: 3.2.46: tagged laces to
  tie hose to doublet.

policy: for policy: as a tactic.

politicly: cunningly.

porringer: basin.

port: 1.1.201, 3.1.35: status.

possession: in possession: on
  marriage.

practise on: trick.

prate: talk foolishly.

preposterous: perverse, putting
  last what should be first.

prerogative: precedence.

present (adj.): immediate;
  presently: at once.

pricked in't: pinned to it;
  pricks him: incites him.

prithee: I pray thee: please.

proceeder: 4.2.11: (a) academic
  aspirant; (b) amatory venturer.

prodigy: omen.

proof: is sorted to no proof:
  comes to nothing; to the proof:
  with the utmost strength.

proper stripling: handsome
  youth.

prove: 2.1.144-5: (a) become;
  (b) test; prove upon thee:
  prove by fighting you.

pumps: soft shoes.

put her down: 5.2.35-6:
  (a) defeat her; (b) copulate
  with her.

quaff carouses: drink toasts.

quaint: (i: 3.2.141: a) clever;
  (b) prim; (ii: 4.3.102: a)
  dainty; (b) prim.

quit: be quit with: 3.1.90: (a)
  retaliate against; (b) be rid of.

rail (vb.): be abusive.

ranging: 3.1.89: (a) straying;
  (b) being inconstant.

rate (vb.): berate, rebuke.

rayed: (i: 3.2.50: a) discoloured; (b) streaked; (ii: 4.1.3:) dirtied.

rebused: (error for) abused.

repute you: esteem you.

resolve (vb.): 4.2.7: inform.

rests: 1.1.243: remains.

roe: small deer.

rope-tricks: (perhaps) showy rhetoric.

roundly: (i: 3.2.207:) strongly, boldly; (ii: 5.2.21-2: a) boldly; (b) with rotundity; **come roundly:** speak plainly; **roundly go about:** boldly tackle.

rout (noun): crowd.

rudesby: ruffian.

ruff: starched frilly neckpiece.

ruffling: (perhaps) ornate.

rush-candle: candle made by dipping a rush in grease.

saciety: satiety.

sack (noun): white wine.

sadness: in good sadness: in all seriousness.

Saint Jeronimie: (confusion of) St Jerome and Kyd's Hieronimo.

scape: escape; **scapes:** 5.2.3: (a) escapades; (b) escapes.

scold (noun): cantankerous woman.

score (noun): (i: Ind.2.22:) list of debts; (ii: 2.1.351:) twenty.

score (vb.): mark.

scrivener: notary.

scuse: excuse.

seal: sealed quart: quart pot marked to guarantee its volume; **seal the title:** confirm the ownership.

secret: 1.1.151: intimately trusted.

secure: carefree.

sedges: water-reeds.

seen: 1.2.131: qualified.

Semiramis: legendary lustful queen.

sensible: (i: 4.1.57: a) capable of being felt; (b) rational; (c) striking; (d) painful; (ii: 5.2.18: a) judicious; (b) rational.

serve in: serve up.

sessa: Ind.1.5: (perhaps: a) from *cesa* (Sp.): stop; (b) from *cessez* (Fr.): stop; (c) from *c'est ça* (Fr.): that's it.

sharp: famished.

sheathing: being fitted with a sheath.

sheer ale: Ind.2.22: (a) undiluted ale; (b) weak ale; (c) ale without food.

shift (noun): trick, stratagem.

shipping: 5.1.35: voyage, i.e. marriage.

shoulder-shotten: with a strained or dislocated shoulder.

shrew: cantankerous person.

shrewd: sharp-tongued.

Sibyl: the Cumæan Sibyl, an agèd seer.

simple: 5.2.161: naïve.

sirrah (to an inferior): lad, fellow.

sith: since.

six-score: 120.

skills (vb.): matters.

skipper: 2.1.332: (a) scamp, gadabout; (b) sailor, roamer.

slickly: sleekly.

slipped: 5.2.52: unleashed.

small ale: cheap weak ale.

soft, softly: 1.2.233; 4.4.23: be patient.

sol-fa (vb.): 1.2.17: (a) use the notes of the musical scale; (b) cry out in pain.

something (adv.): somewhat.

sooth: truth; good sooth: yes indeed.

sop: piece of bread soaked in wine.

sounded: 2.1.192-3: (a) proclaimed; (b) tested for depth.

souns: by God's wounds.

spavin: swelling or tumour in the leg.

specialties: specific contracts.

sped: done for, defeated; sped with spavins: ruined by swellings in the legs.

speed: 2.1.138: (a) progress; (b) prosperity; speeding: 2.1.294: prospering.

spleen: (i: Ind.1.134:) source of mirth; (ii: 3.2.10:) bad-tempered waywardness.

sportful: amorously playful.

staggers (noun): disease causing giddiness.

stale (noun): (i: 1.1.58: a) laughing-stock; (b) whore; (c) cat's-paw; (d) stalemate; (ii: 3.1.88: a) decoy, lure; (b) tempter.

stand: 1.2.152: (a) remain; (b) be sexually tumescent; stands: Ind.2.119-20: (a) suffices; (b) is erect.

starved: App.19: (a) dead of cold; (b) dead of hunger.

stay: delay; stayed: detained; stays thy leisure: awaits your convenience.

stead (vb.): serve.

stock: (i: 1.1.31:) blockhead; (ii: 3.2.62:) stocking (long sock).

Stoics: philosophers advocating indifference to pleasure.

stomach: (i: 1.1.38; 1.2.191:) inclination; (ii: 4.1.143:) appetite.

stoop: 4.1.176: (a) swoop to a lure; (b) submit to my will.

straight (adv.): immediately.

strange: 1.1.85: distant, unfriendly.

stripling: proper stripling: handsome youth.

stuff: Ind.2.133-4: (a) matter; (b) furnishings.

suffer: 2.1.31: allow.

suits: Ind.1.103: (a) respects; (b) outfits.

supposes: counterfeit supposes: false notions.

swayed: 3.2.52: strained and sagging or crooked.

sweeting: sweet-heart.

swinge: beat.

take: take it on you: assume your authority; take upon you: play your part.

tales: 2.1.215: (a) unlikely notions; (b) 'tails', genitalia; (c) 'tails', anal areas.

tall: 4.4.17: capable.

tane: taken, caught.

tapster: barman, waiter.

tents: 2.1.345: tent-like bed-canopies.

think on: remember.

thirdborough: constable.

this's a heavy chance: this is a sad incident.

thou't: thou wilt: you will.

thralled: captivated.

throat: **lies in's throat**: is utterly false.

throughly: thoroughly.

tight: 2.1.372: water-tight, sound.

tilly vally: nonsense.

time: 4.3.69: fashion; **in good time**: indeed.

to: 3.2.151: compared to.

toward (adj.): (i: 1.1.68; 5.1.12:) impending; (ii: 5.2.182:) compliant.

toy: trivial item.

traffic: trade.

trapped: fitted with trappings.

trencher: wooden dish.

trick: trifle.

tripe: pale meat from an animal's stomach.

trot (noun): hag.

trow: (i: 1.2.4:) believe; (1.2.161:) know.

trunk (adj.): full.

tumbling-trick: acrobatic performance.

turn: **for your turn**: for your needs, particularly sexual; **serve the turn**: suffice for the purpose; **thrice turned**: turned inside out three times.

turtle: turtle-dove.

tut: interjection of impatience.

Tyrian: made in Tyre, a Syrian port famed for red dye.

unapt: unfitted.

uncase thee: remove your outer clothes.

undertake: assume, adopt.

undone: 5.1.55-6: ruined.

unkind: 5.2.136: (a) unnatural; (b) hostile.

unpinked: not decorated by perforations.

untoward: stubborn.

use: 4.3.152-4: (a) business; (b) sexual act.

vail your stomachs: suppress your pride.

vallens: 2.1.347: valances: canopy-fringes.

vantage: opportunity.

velure: velour: velvety fabric.

vent (vb.): proclaim.

veriest: truest, most extreme.

very: **very a fool**: truly a fool; **very name**: name alone.

vied: 2.1.302: added.

vilde: vile.

vouchsafe: deign.

want: 3.2.5: lack; **wants**: 3.2.239, 241: are lacking.

wanton (adj.): erotic.

warrant (vb.): promise, assure.

watch: 4.1.180: keep awake; **watch our vantage**: seek our opportunity.

ways: **foul ways**: vile roads.

wear: 3.2.112: wear down; **wears**: 3.2.105: passes.

welkin: sky.

wench (colloquial): young woman.

what: 4.1.77: why.

when?: 4.1.128, 129: hurry up!

where away?: where are you going?

whit: tiny bit.

white: **hit the white**: 5.2.186: (a) hit the target; (b) won Bianca.

whoreson (adj.): low-born (son of a whore).

widowhood: estate allotted at marriage for a wife's widowhood.

will you, nill you: willy-nilly,
  inevitably.
windgall: tumour on leg.
withal: (i: 1.2.80, 4.5.49:) with
  it; (ii: 1.2.113, 4.2.31, 5.1.16,
  18:) with; (iii: 3.1.60:) too;
  (iv: 3.2.25:) nevertheless.
witness: with a witness:
  deliberately.
woodcock: 1.2.157: (a) bird
  deemed stupid; (b) fool.
wonderful: incredible, amazing.
world: 'tis a world: It's worth
  a world.
worthy: of worthy memory:
  well worth remembering.
wrong: the more my wrong:
  the more I am wronged.
yellows: jaundice.
yard: wooden measure, three
  feet (*c.* 91 cm.) in length.
yet: Ind.2.65: still.
youngling: 2.1.330: (a) little
  youth; (b) novice.
Zentippe: Xanthippe, shrewish
  wife of Socrates.